Data Modelling and Design
Based on CDMP

Colophon

Title: Data Modelling and Design

Subtitle: Based on CDMP

Authors: Michel Dekker

Publisher: Van Haren Publishing, ‘s-Hertogenbosch

ISBN Paperback: 978 94 018 1378 5

Edition: Design: First edition, first print, October, 2025

For further information about Van Haren Publishing please e-mail us at: info@vanharen.net or visit our website: www.vanharen.net

Publisher about the Courseware

The Courseware was created by experts from the industry who served as the author(s) for this publication. The input for the material is based on existing publications and the experience and expertise of the author(s). The material has been revised by trainers who also have experience working with the material. Close attention was also paid to the key learning points to ensure what needs to be mastered.

The objective of the courseware is to provide maximum support to the trainer and to the student, during his or her training. The material has a modular structure and according to the author(s) has the highest success rate should the student opt for examination. The Courseware is also accredited for this reason, wherever applicable.

In order to satisfy the requirements for accreditation the material must meet certain quality standards. The structure, the use of certain terms, diagrams and references are all part of this accreditation. Additionally, the material must be made available to each student in order to obtain full accreditation. To optimally support the trainer and the participant of the training assignments, practice exams and results are provided with the material.

Direct reference to advised literature is also regularly covered in the sheets so that students can find additional information concerning a particular topic. The decision to leave out notes pages from the Courseware was to encourage students to take notes throughout the material. Although the courseware is complete, the possibility that the trainer deviates from the structure of the sheets or chooses to not refer to all the sheets or commands does exist. The student always has the possibility to cover these topics and go through them on their own time. It is recommended to follow the structure of the courseware and publications for maximum exam preparation.

The courseware and the recommended literature are the perfect combination to learn and understand the theory.

-- Van Haren Publishing

Other publications BY Van Haren Publishing

Van Haren Publishing (VHP) specializes in titles on Best Practices, methods, frameworks and standards within four domains:
- IT Management
- Architecture (Enterprise and IT)
- Business Management and
- Project Management

Van Haren Publishing is publishing on behalf of leading organizations and companies: Agile Consortium, World Commerce and Contracting, IAOP, IPMA World, KNVI, PMI-NL, NLAIC and The Open Group.

Van Haren Publishing is part of the Van Haren Group and additional to the book publishing also provides the following services: accredited training materials and e-learning through Van Haren Learning Solutions, as well as independent professional certification via examination through Van Haren Certify.

Topics are (per domain):

IT Management	IT Service Management	FitSM, ISM®, ISO/IEC20000, IT4IT®, ITIL®, VerISM®, SAF, TRIM, XLA®
	Data Management	Data literacy, Data visualization, DMBOK
	IT Asset Management	HAM, ITAM, SAM
	IT Security Management	BIO, ISO/IEC27001, NIS2
	Test Management	CTAP
	Application Management	ASL
	Other	eCF, IT-CMF, Scrum
Project Management	Project Management	Half Double, ICB, ISO/IEC21500, P3.express, PM2, PMBOK Guide, Praxis, PRINCE2
	Agile	Agile, Agile PM
	Other	PMO
Business Management	Operations Management	Lean, Lean Six Sigma, OBM, OMC, RASCI
	Contract Management	CATS CM, CATS RVM, IACCM World
	Business Information Management	BiSL, DID
	Artificial Intelligence	AI, Generative AI
	Outsourcing	OPBOK
Enterprise Architecture	Enterprise Architecture	BIAN, TOGAF
	Modeling	ArchiMate, BPMN
	Software Architecture	ISAQB
	Other	Open Agile Architecture

For the latest information on VHP publications, visit our website: www.vanharen.net.

Table of Content

Self-Reflection of understanding Diagram

'What you do not measure, you cannot control.'' – Tom Peters

Fill in this diagram to self-evaluate your understanding of the material. This is an evaluation of how well you know the material and how well you understand it. In order to pass the exam successfully you should be aiming to reach the higher end of Level 3. If you really want to become a pro, then you should be aiming for Level 4. Your overall level of understanding will naturally follow the learning curve. So, it's important to keep track of where you are at each point of the training and address any areas of difficulty.

Based on where you are within the Self-Reflection of Understanding diagram you can evaluate the progress of your own training.

Level of Understanding	Before Training (Pre-knowledge)	Training Part 1 (1st Half)	raining Part 2 (2nd Half)	After studying / reading the book	After exercises and the Practice exam
Level 4 I can explain the content and apply it .					
Level 3 I get it! I am right where I am supposed to be.					Ready for the exam!
Level 2 I almost have it but could use more practice.					
Level 1 I am learning but don't quite get it yet.					

(Self-Reflection of Understanding Diagram)

Write down the problem areas that you are still having difficulty with so that you can consolidate them yourself, or with your trainer. After you have had a look at these, then you should evaluate to see if you now have a better understanding of where you actually are on the learning curve.

Troubleshooting

Problem areas:	***Topic:***
Part 1	
Part 2	
You have gone through the book and studied.	
You have answered the questions and done the practice exam.	

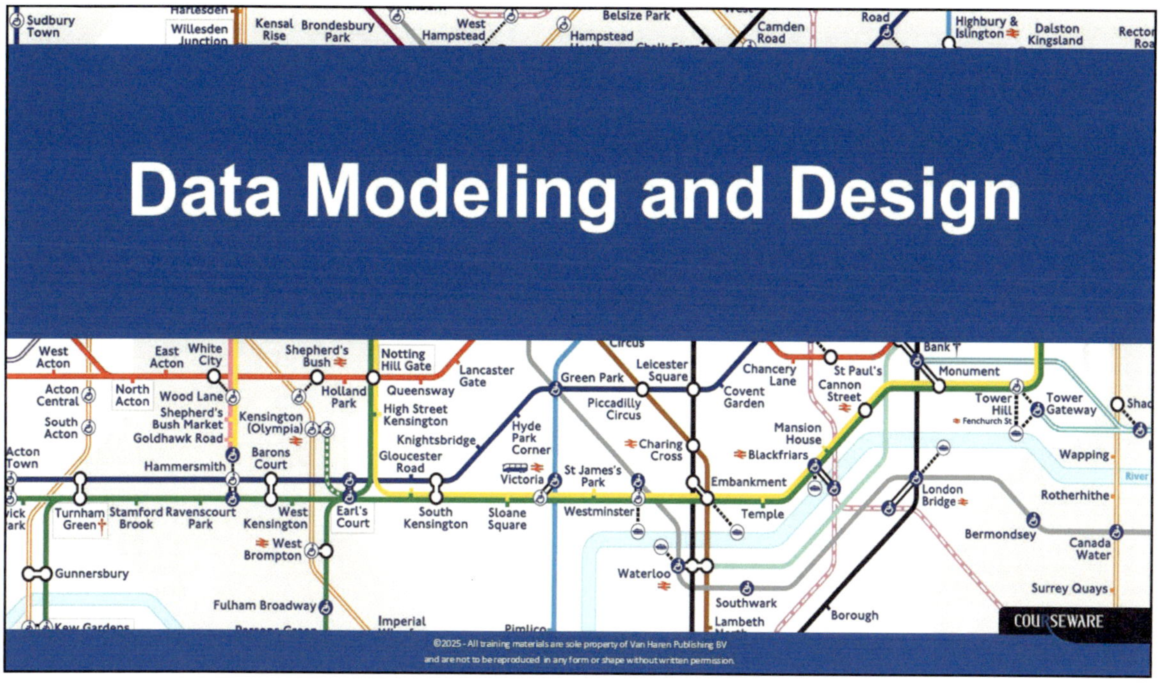

Effective Data Foundation

Not-for-profit collective, which enables **professionals** to **leverage data** to make **sustainable business decisions**

© Van Haren Publishing 2

Effective Data Foundation
DATA
Analysis / Literacy / Management / Visualization
© Van Haren Publishing
3

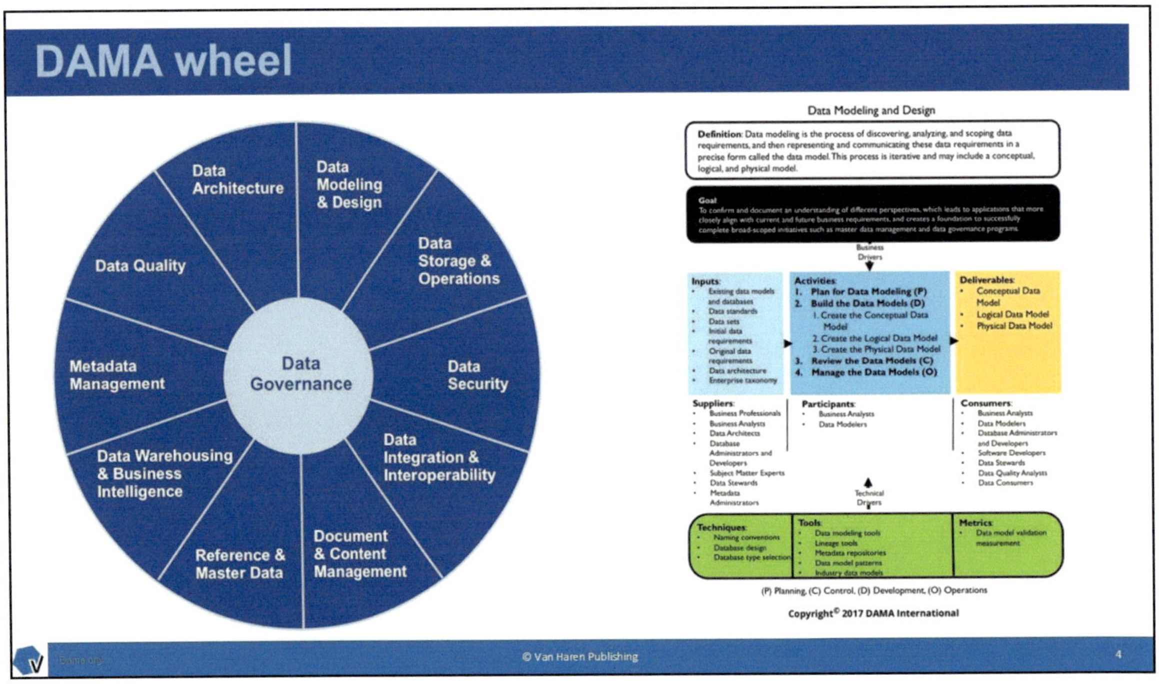
DAMA wheel
Data Architecture
Data Modeling & Design
Data Storage & Operations
Data Security
Data Integration & Interoperability
Document & Content Management
Reference & Master Data
Data Warehousing & Business Intelligence
Metadata Management
Data Quality
Data Governance
Data Modeling and Design
Definition: Data modeling is the process of discovering, analyzing, and scoping data requirements, and then representing and communicating these data requirements in a precise form called the data model. This process is iterative and may include a conceptual, logical, and physical model.
Goal:
To confirm and document an understanding of different perspectives, which leads to applications that more closely align with current and future business requirements, and creates a foundation to successfully complete broad-scoped initiatives such as master data management and data governance programs.
Business Drivers
Inputs:
Existing data models and databases
Data standards
Data sets
Initial data requirements
Original data requirements
Data architecture
Enterprise taxonomy
Activities:
1. Plan for Data Modeling (P)
2. Build the Data Models (D)
1. Create the Conceptual Data Model
2. Create the Logical Data Model
3. Create the Physical Data Model
3. Review the Data Models (C)
4. Manage the Data Models (O)
Deliverables:
Conceptual Data Model
Logical Data Model
Physical Data Model
Suppliers:
Business Professionals
Business Analysts
Data Architects
Database Administrators and Developers
Subject Matter Experts
Data Stewards
Metadata Administrators
Participants:
Business Analysts
Data Modelers
Consumers:
Business Analysts
Data Modelers
Database Administrators and Developers
Software Developers
Data Stewards
Data Quality Analysts
Data Consumers
Technical Drivers
Techniques:
Naming conventions
Database design
Database type selection
Tools:
Data modeling tools
Lineage tools
Metadata repositories
Data model patterns
Industry data models
Metrics:
Data model validation measurement
(P) Planning, (C) Control, (D) Development, (O) Operations
Copyright© 2017 DAMA International
© Van Haren Publishing
4

Certification
ASSOCIATE
PRACTITIONER
MASTER
FELLOW
CDMP Associate
CDMP Practitioner
CDMP Master
CDMP Fellow
Membership
Central
Industry experience
6 months > 5 years
Requirements
60% pass
Data Management
Fundamentals exam
Membership
Central
Industry experience
2 years - 10 years
Requirements
70% pass in
Data Management
Fundamentals exam
and 70% pass in 2
specialist exams
Membership
Central
Industry experience
Minimum 10 years^
Requirements
80% pass in
Data Management
Fundamentals exam
and 80% pass in 2
specialist exams
Membership
Central
Industry experience
25 years plus
Requirements
Globally recognised &
respected thought
leadership
Significant contribution
to Data Management
profession
CDMP Master
Contribution to CDMP &
DMBOK
By nomination
© Van Haren Publishing
5

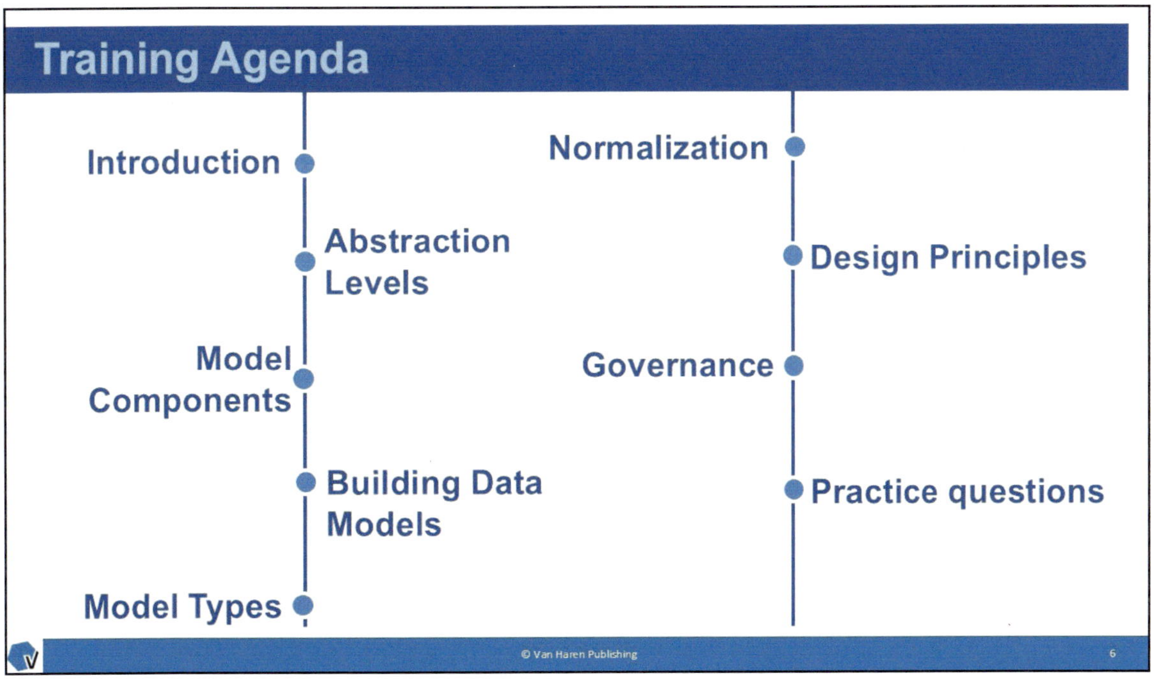
Training Agenda
Introduction
Abstraction Levels
Model Components
Building Data Models
Model Types
Normalization
Design Principles
Governance
Practice questions
© Van Haren Publishing
6

Introduction

The main purpose of a data model is not to design a database, but to ***describe a business***

C. Bradley, CDMP Fellow 2010

What is a Model?

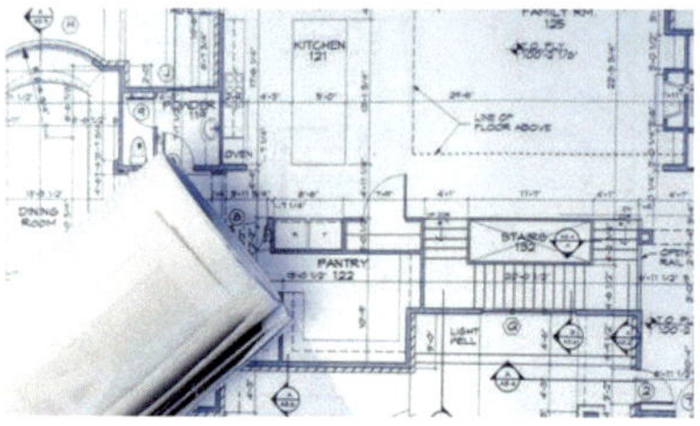

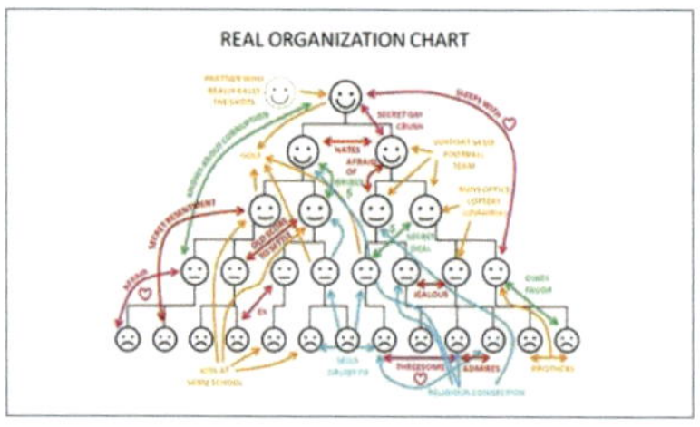

What is Data Modeling?

The process of **discovering, analyzing and scoping** data requirements,

and then **representing and communicating** these requirements

in a **data model**

Business Drivers

Return on Modeling Effort

- **R** Common vocabulary
- **O** Capturing knowledge
- **M** Improve communication
- **E** Starting point for changes

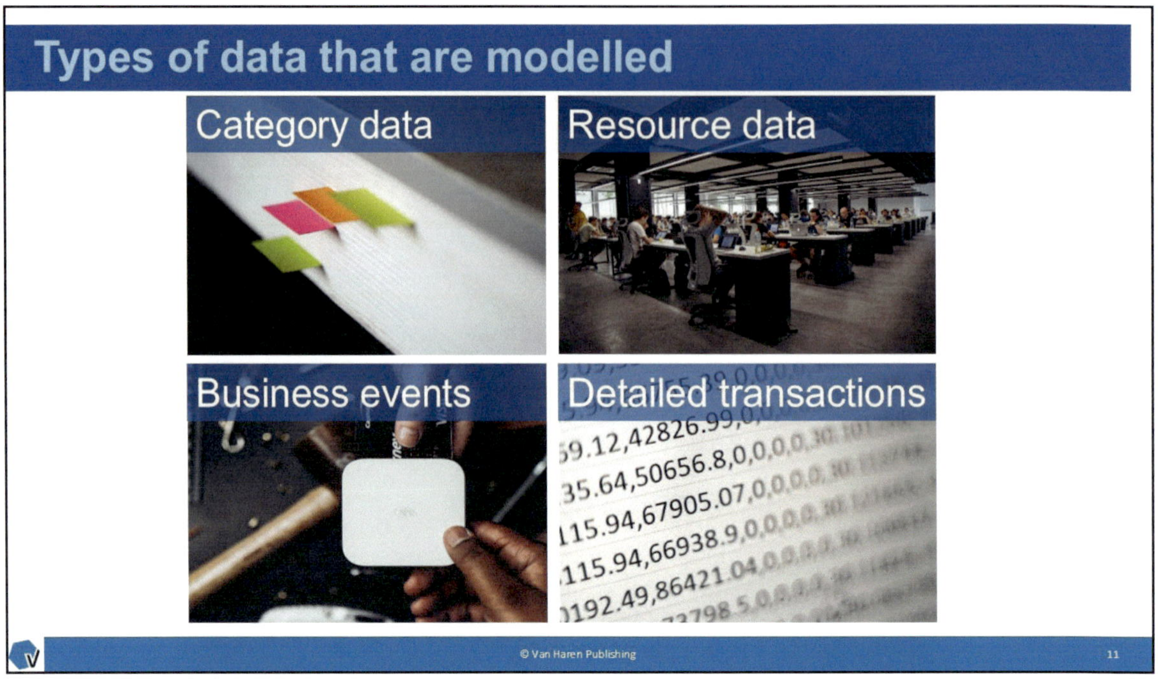
Types of data that are modelled
Category data
Resource data
Business events
Detailed transactions
© Van Haren Publishing
11

Abstraction levels
If you can't explain it simply, you don't understand it well enough.
(probably not) Albert Einstein
© Van Haren Publishing
12

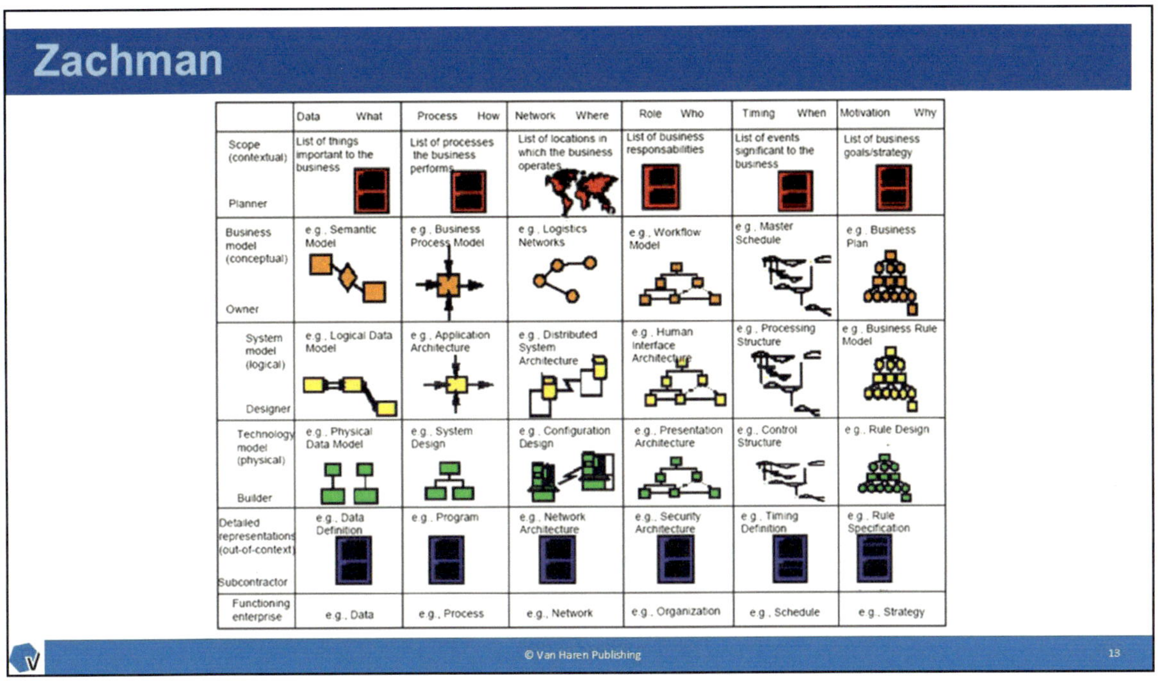

	Data What	Process How	Network Where	Role Who	Timing When	Motivation Why
Scope (contextual) Planner	List of things important to the business	List of processes the business performs	List of locations in which the business operates	List of business responsabilities	List of events significant to the business	List of business goals/strategy
Business model (conceptual) Owner	e.g. Semantic Model	e.g. Business Process Model	e.g. Logistics Networks	e.g. Workflow Model	e.g. Master Schedule	e.g. Business Plan
System model (logical) Designer	e.g. Logical Data Model	e.g. Application Architecture	e.g. Distributed System Architecture	e.g. Human Interface Architecture	e.g. Processing Structure	e.g. Business Rule Model
Technology model (physical) Builder	e.g. Physical Data Model	e.g. System Design	e.g. Configuration Design	e.g. Presentation Architecture	e.g. Control Structure	e.g. Rule Design
Detailed representations (out-of-context) Subcontractor	e.g. Data Definition	e.g. Program	e.g. Network Architecture	e.g. Security Architecture	e.g. Timing Definition	e.g. Rule Specification
Functioning enterprise	e.g. Data	e.g. Process	e.g. Network	e.g. Organization	e.g. Schedule	e.g. Strategy

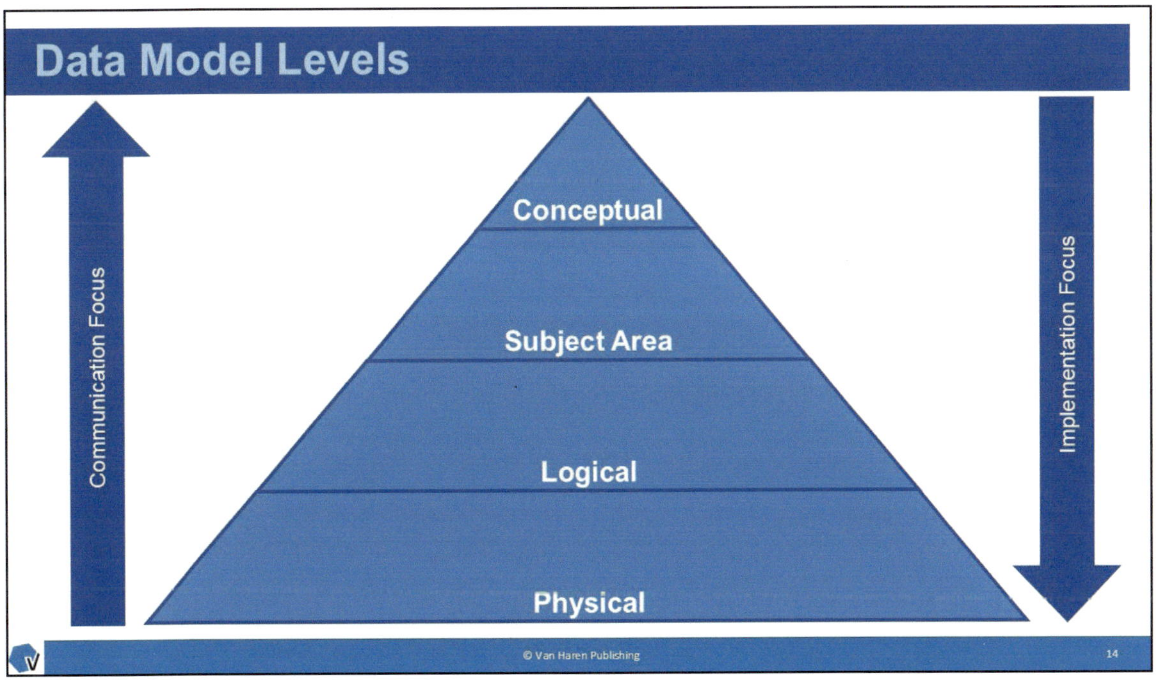

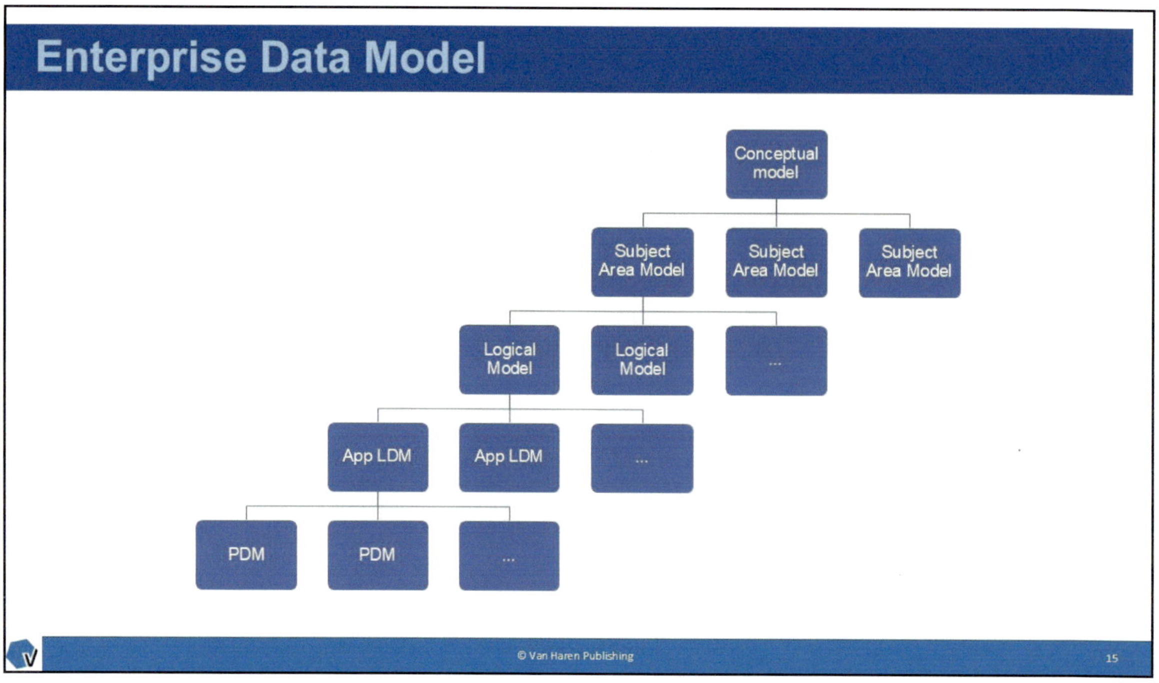
Enterprise Data Model
Conceptual model
Subject Area Model
Subject Area Model
Subject Area Model
Logical Model
Logical Model
...
App LDM
App LDM
...
PDM
PDM
...
© Van Haren Publishing
15

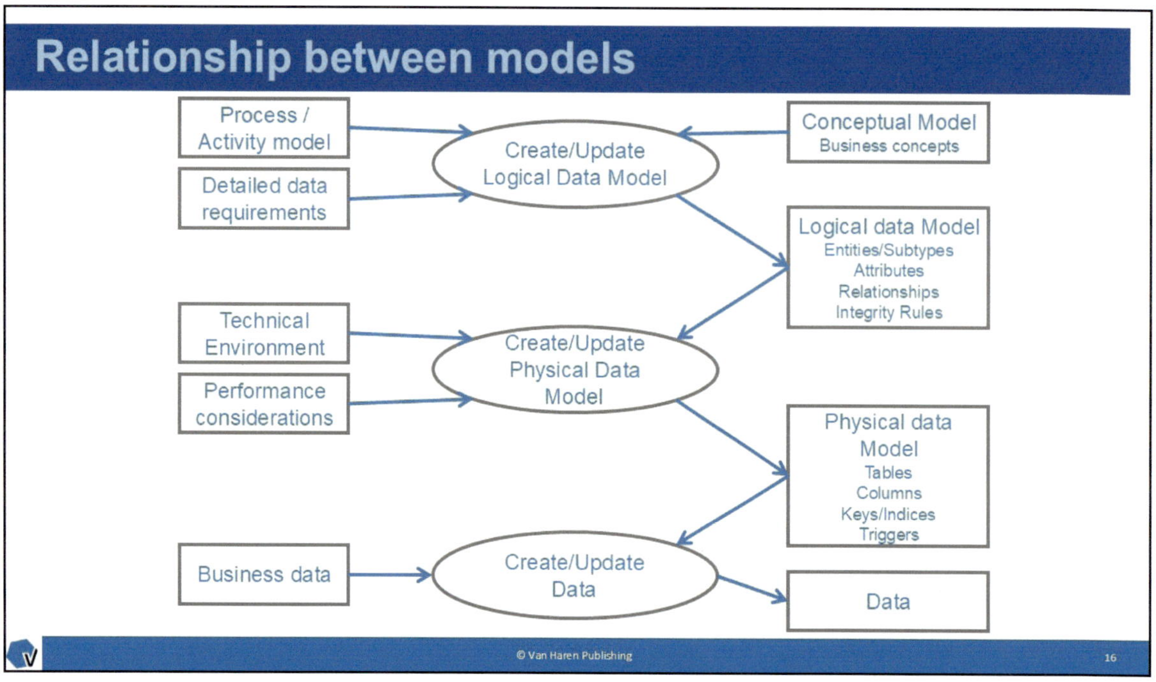
Relationship between models
Process / Activity model
Detailed data requirements
Create/Update Logical Data Model
Conceptual Model
Business concepts
Logical data Model
Entities/Subtypes
Attributes
Relationships
Integrity Rules
Technical Environment
Performance considerations
Create/Update Physical Data Model
Physical data Model
Tables
Columns
Keys/Indices
Triggers
Business data
Create/Update Data
Data
© Van Haren Publishing
16

Conceptual data model

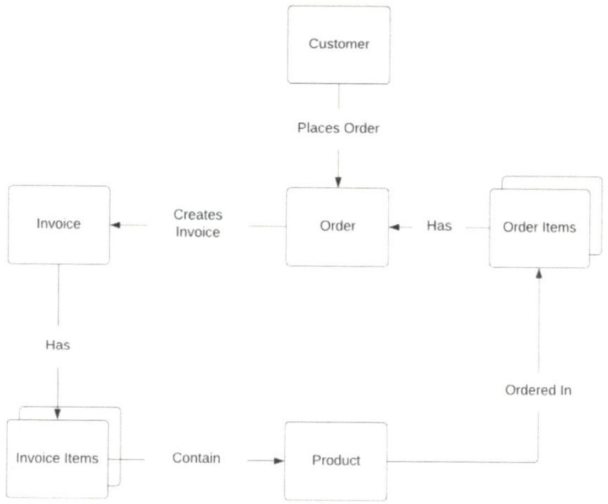

Subject Area Model

- Scope
- Abstraction
- Communication
- Understanding
- Foundation for further modeling
- Consistency

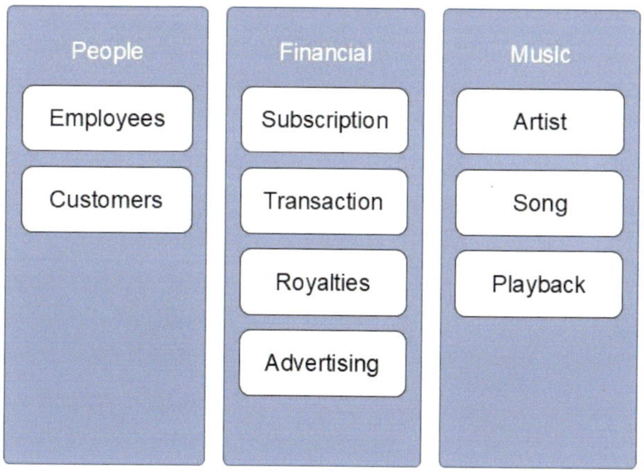

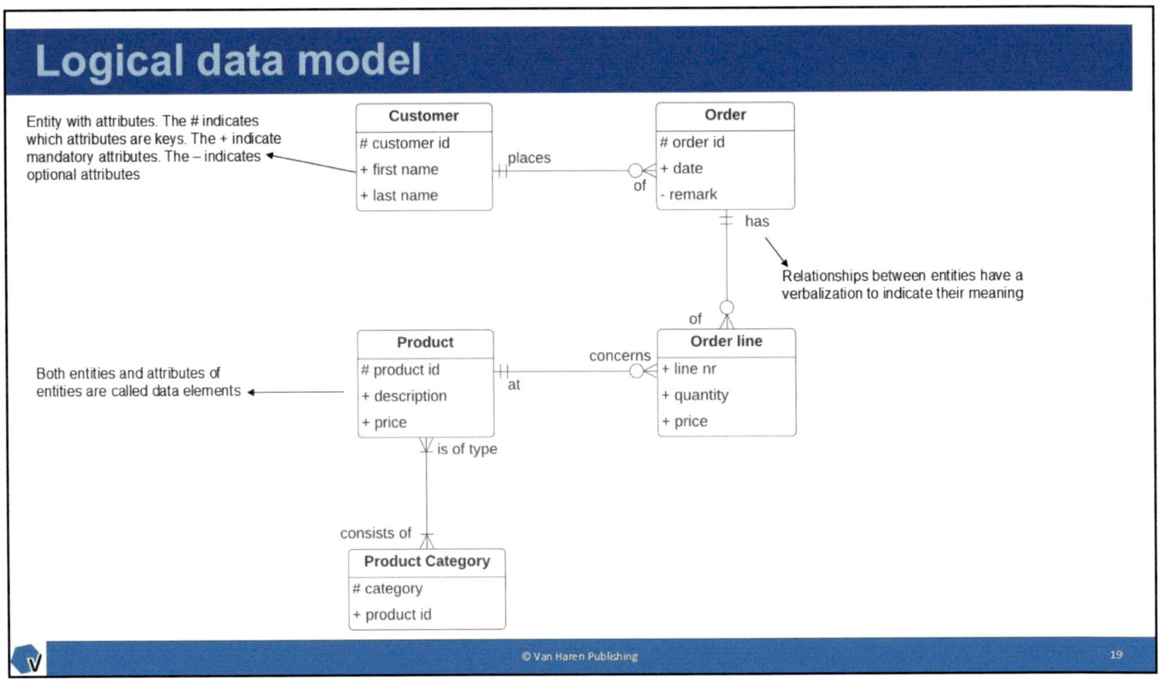
Logical data model
Entity with attributes. The # indicates which attributes are keys. The + indicate mandatory attributes. The – indicates optional attributes
Customer
customer id
+ first name
+ last name
places
of
Order
order id
+ date
- remark
has
Relationships between entities have a verbalization to indicate their meaning
of
Product
product id
+ description
+ price
concerns
at
Order line
+ line nr
+ quantity
+ price
Both entities and attributes of entities are called data elements
is of type
consists of
Product Category
category
+ product id
© Van Haren Publishing
19

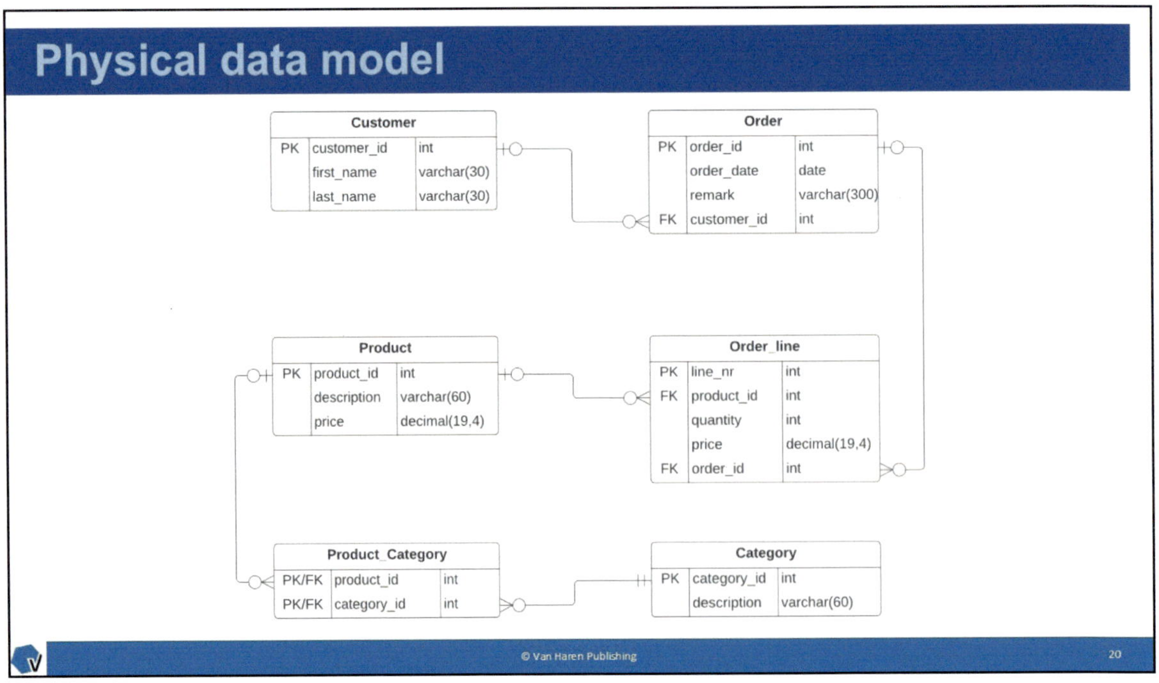
Physical data model
Customer
PK customer_id int
first_name varchar(30)
last_name varchar(30)
Order
PK order_id int
order_date date
remark varchar(300)
FK customer_id int
Product
PK product_id int
description varchar(60)
price decimal(19,4)
Order_line
PK line_nr int
FK product_id int
quantity int
price decimal(19,4)
FK order_id int
Product_Category
PK/FK product_id int
PK/FK category_id int
Category
PK category_id int
description varchar(60)
© Van Haren Publishing
20

Data Model Components

*All models are **wrong**, some are **useful***

George Box, 1976

© Van Haren Publishing 21

Data model components

© Van Haren Publishing 22

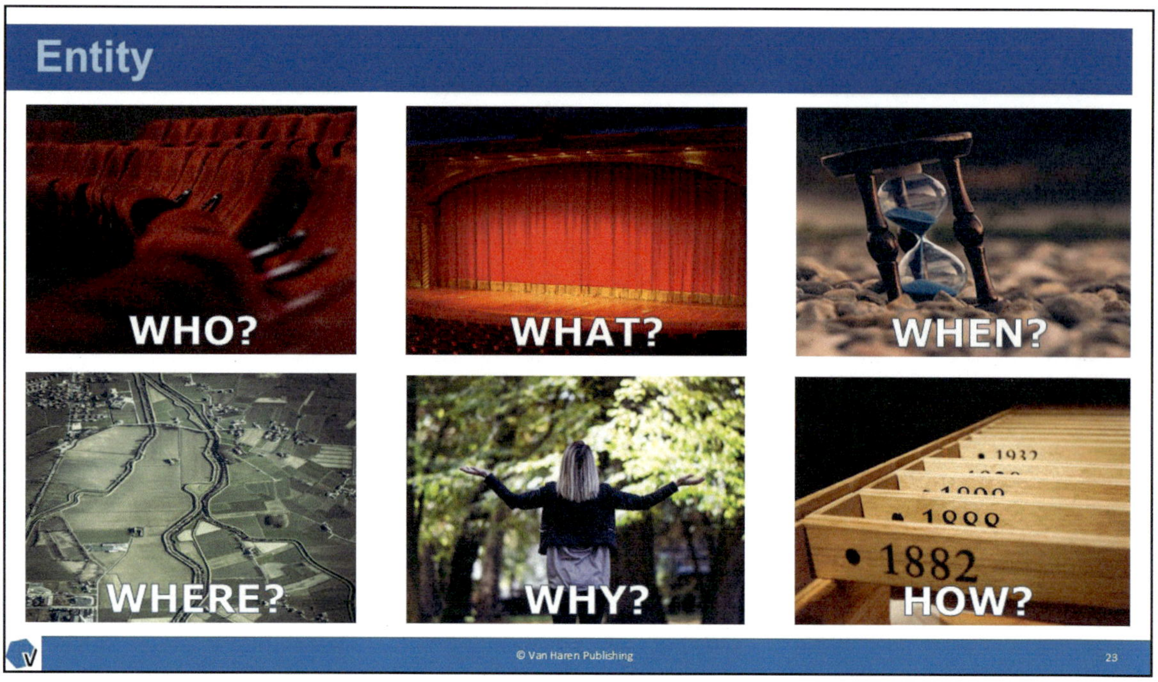

Entity

Artist: A person, or group of persons, who creates, performs or produces music as a profession.

Music Track: A recorded piece of music with melody, rhythm, and instruments.

Consumer: A person who engages with and experiences the auditory and emotional aspect of musical compositions, either by actively choosing to hear them or by passively encountering them. This person has an active *subscription* to a *music platform*.

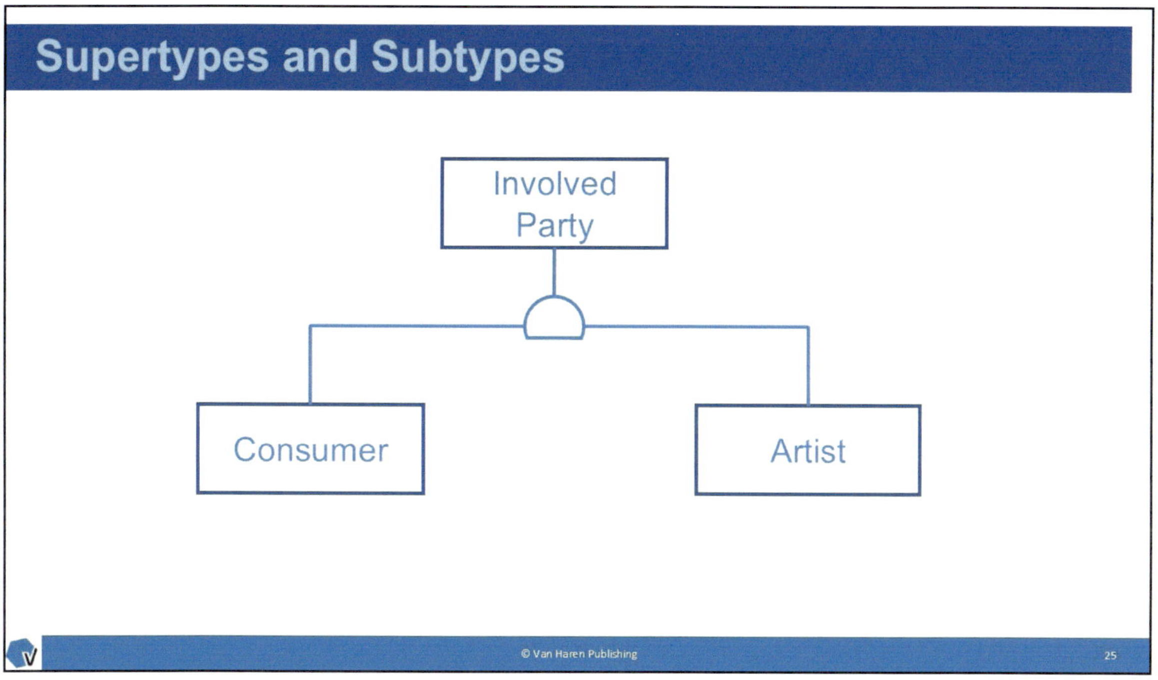
Supertypes and Subtypes
Involved Party
Consumer
Artist
© Van Haren Publishing
25

Relationship
an association between *entities*
© Van Haren Publishing
26

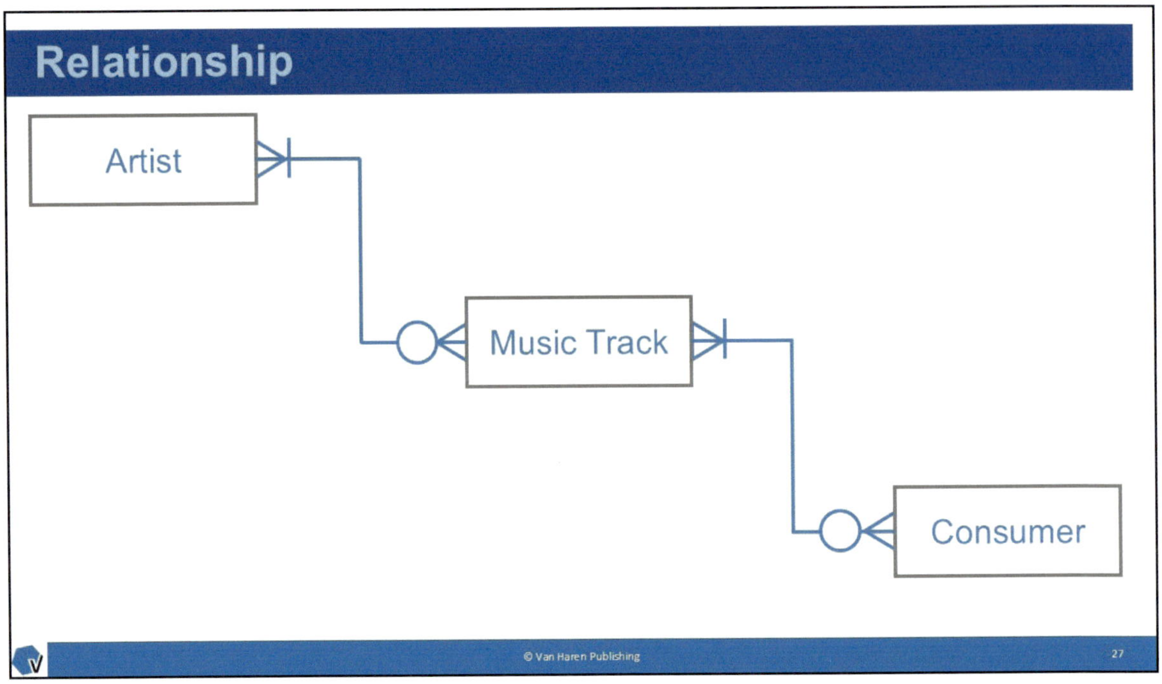
Relationship
Artist
Music Track
Consumer
© Van Haren Publishing
27

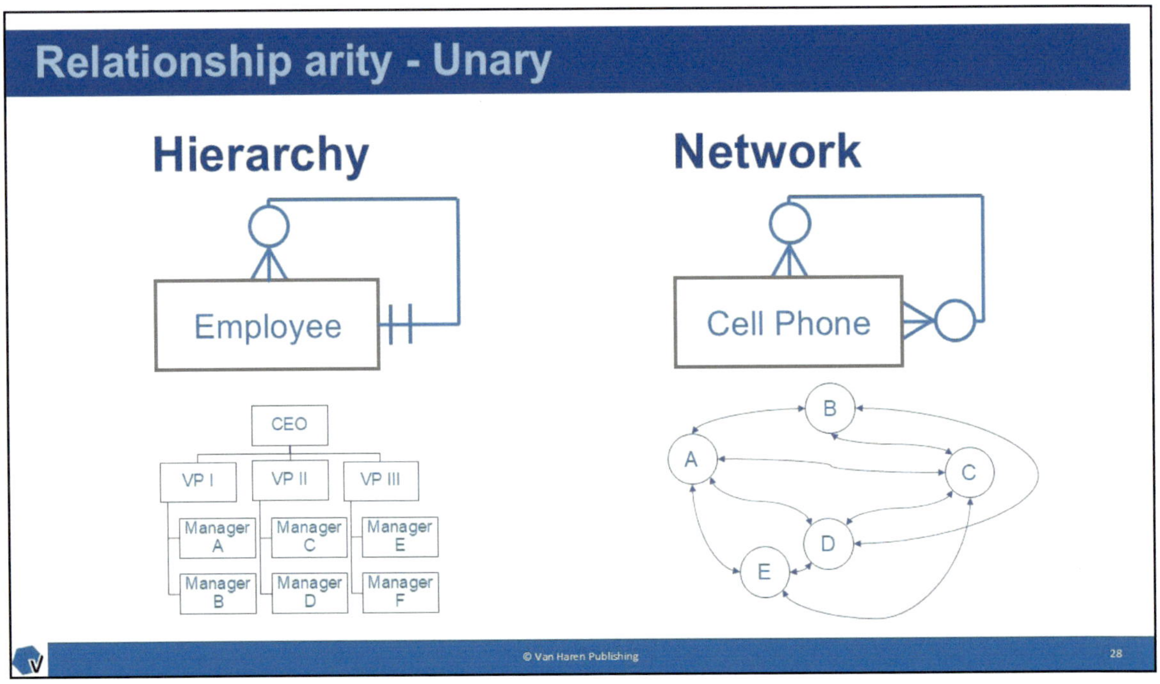
Relationship arity - Unary
Hierarchy
Employee
CEO
VP I
VP II
VP III
Manager A
Manager C
Manager E
Manager B
Manager D
Manager F
Network
Cell Phone
B
A
C
D
E
© Van Haren Publishing
28

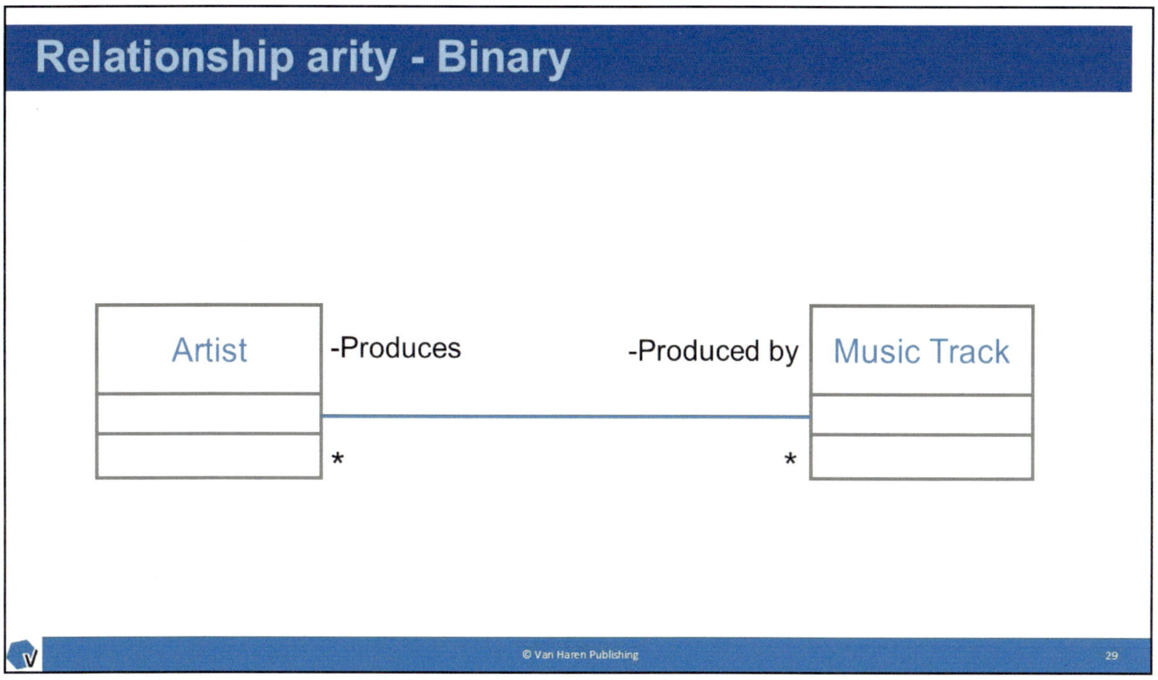
Relationship arity - Binary
Artist
-Produces
-Produced by
Music Track
*
*
© Van Haren Publishing
29

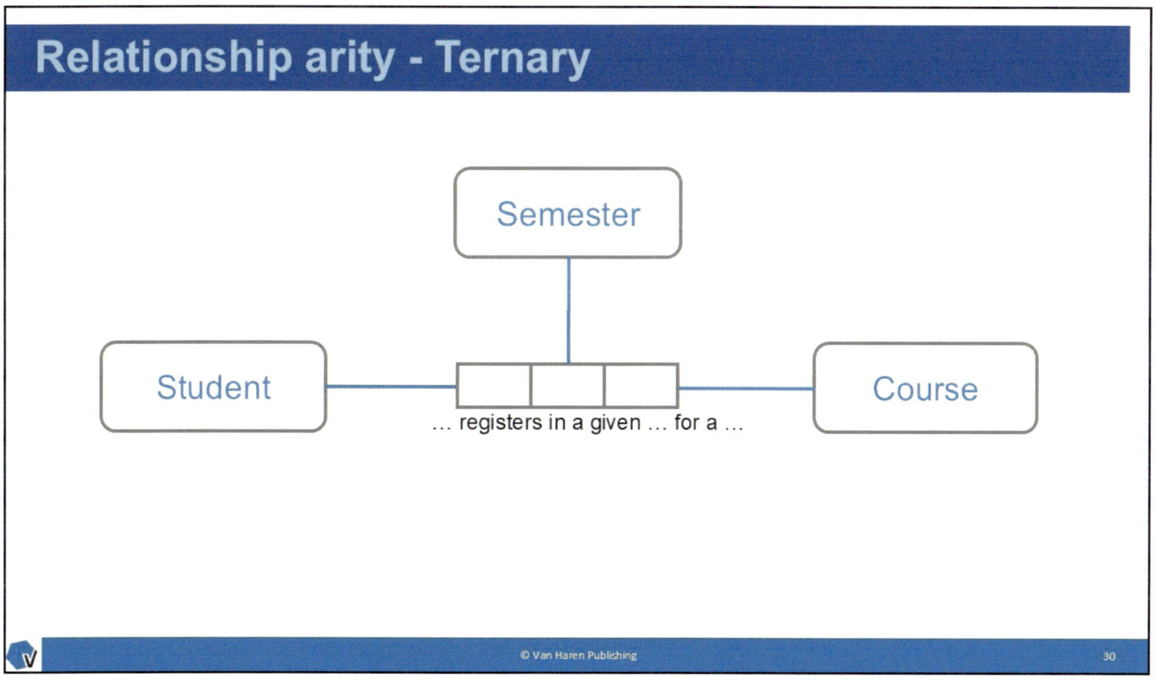
Relationship arity - Ternary
Semester
Student
Course
… registers in a given … for a …
© Van Haren Publishing
30

Foreign key
used in physical and sometimes logical relational data modeling schemes to represent a *relationship*
© Van Haren Publishing
31

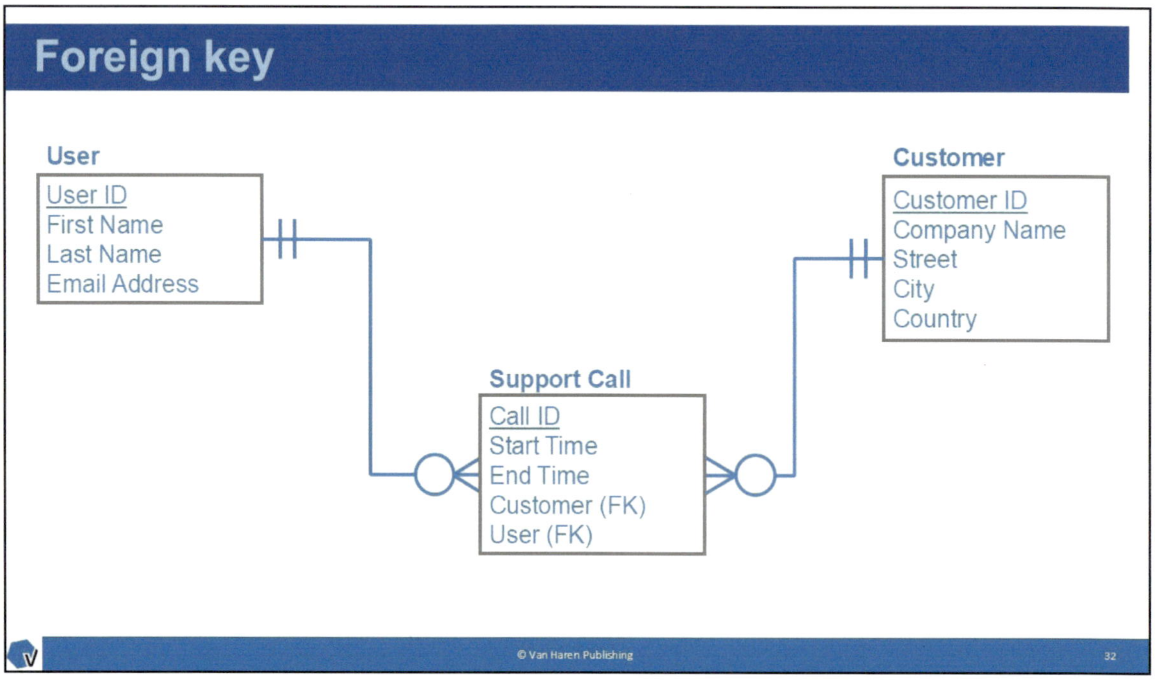
Foreign key
User
User ID
First Name
Last Name
Email Address
Customer
Customer ID
Company Name
Street
City
Country
Support Call
Call ID
Start Time
End Time
Customer (FK)
User (FK)
© Van Haren Publishing
32

Attribute

 33

Attribute

User

User
User ID
First Name
Last Name
Email Address
Login attempts

 34

Identifier or Key
BRITISH PASSPORT
set of one or more *attributes* that uniquely defines an instance of an *entity*
© Van Haren Publishing
35

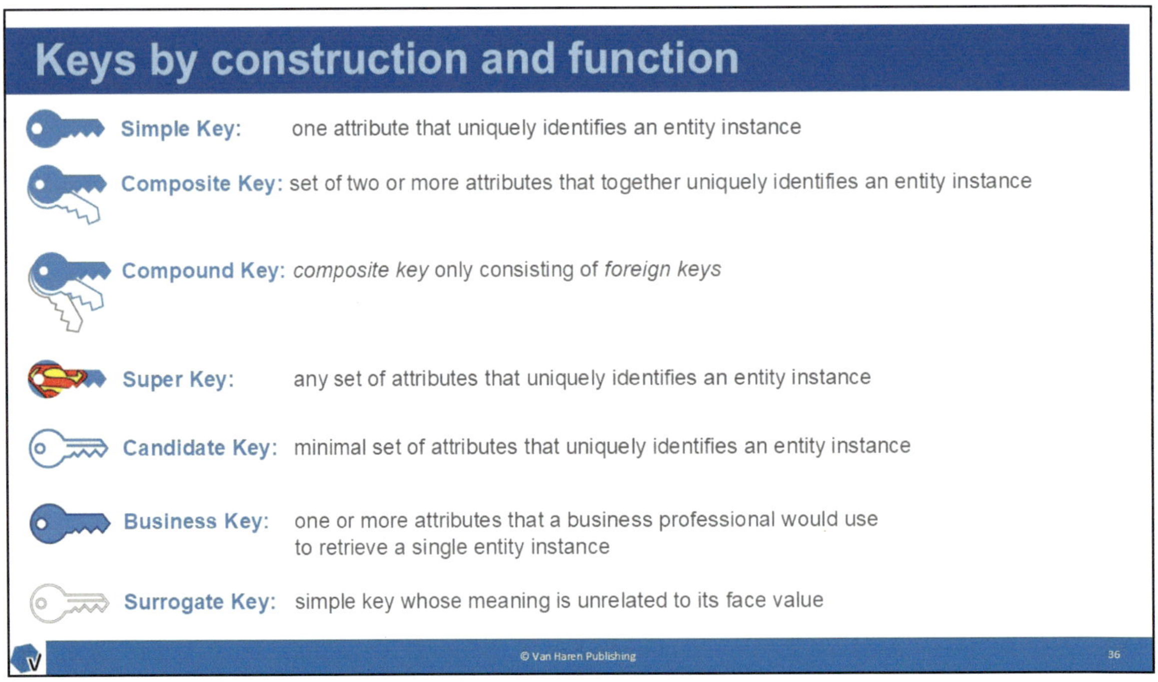
Keys by construction and function
Simple Key: one attribute that uniquely identifies an entity instance
Composite Key: set of two or more attributes that together uniquely identifies an entity instance
Compound Key: *composite key* only consisting of *foreign keys*
Super Key: any set of attributes that uniquely identifies an entity instance
Candidate Key: minimal set of attributes that uniquely identifies an entity instance
Business Key: one or more attributes that a business professional would use to retrieve a single entity instance
Surrogate Key: simple key whose meaning is unrelated to its face value
© Van Haren Publishing
36

Keys by construction and function

Candidate Key: minimal set of attributes that uniquely identifies an entity instance

PK **Primary Key:** *candidate key* that is chosen to be **THE** unique identifier for an entity

AK **Alternate Key:** *candidate key that* although unique, was **NOT** chosen as the *primary key*

Identifying vs. non-identifying relationships

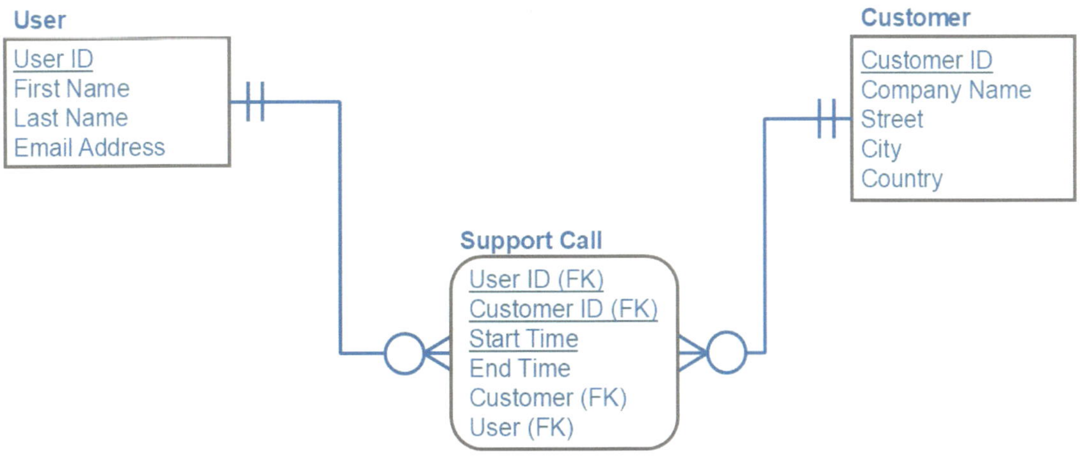

Domain

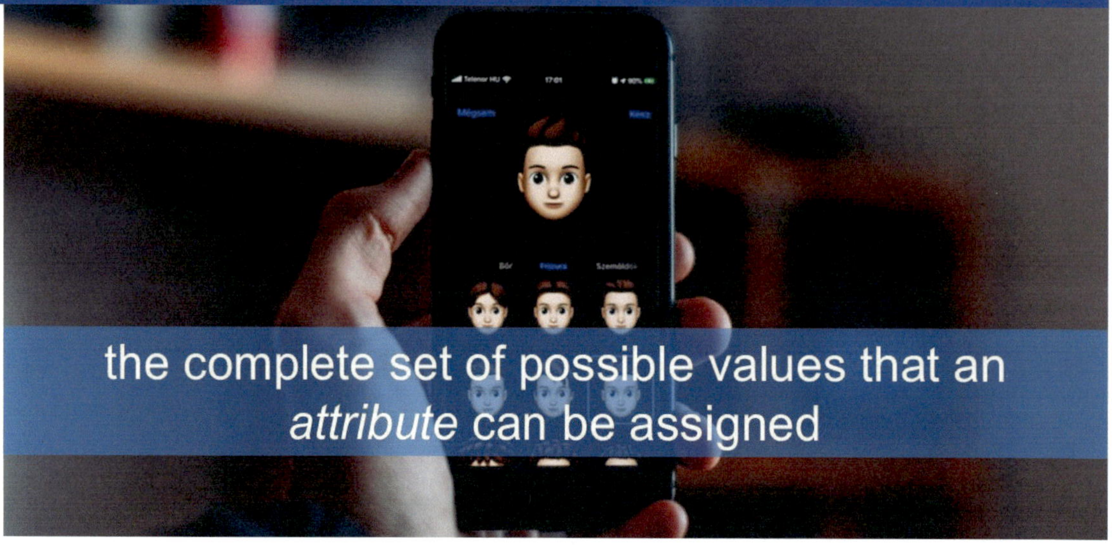

the complete set of possible values that an *attribute* can be assigned

 39

Data types

	SQL Server	Oracle DB
Numeric	INT BIGINT SMALLINT TINYINT DECIMAL FLOAT REAL MONEY SMALLMONEY	NUMBER INTEGER FLOAT BINARY_FLOAT BINARY_DOUBLE
Character Strings	CHAR VARCHAR TEXT NCHAR NVARCHAR NTEXT	CHAR VARCHAR2 NCHAR NVARCHAR2 CLOB NCLOB
Date and Time	DATE TIME DATETIME SMALLDATETIME DATETIME2 DATETIMEOFFSET	DATE TIMESTAMP TIMESTAMP WITH TIME ZONE TIMESTAMP WITH LOCAL TIME ZONE INTERVAL YEAR TO MONTH INTERVAL DAY TO SECOND
Binary Data	BINARY VARBINARY IMAGE	RAW BLOB
Boolean	BIT	BOOLEAN
Other	UNIQUEIDENTIFIER XML	BINARY_INTEGER

 40

Cardinality & notations

describes a fundamental relationship between two entities. There are three types: ***one-to-one***, ***one-to-many***, *and* ***many-to-many***

Leigh van der Veen

 41

Entity Relationship Symbols

Data Model Notation	Representation	Description
Boxes		Entity
Lines		Relationship between two entities
Dotted Lines		Non-identifying relationship
Solid Lines		Identifying relationship
Crow's feet		"Many" (>1) in an N-to-many relationship
Bar		Mandatory relationship (1 or more instances)
Option		Optional relationship (zero or more instances)

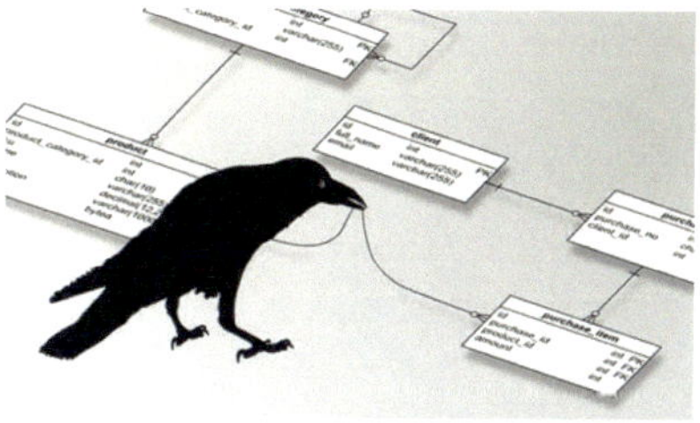

 42

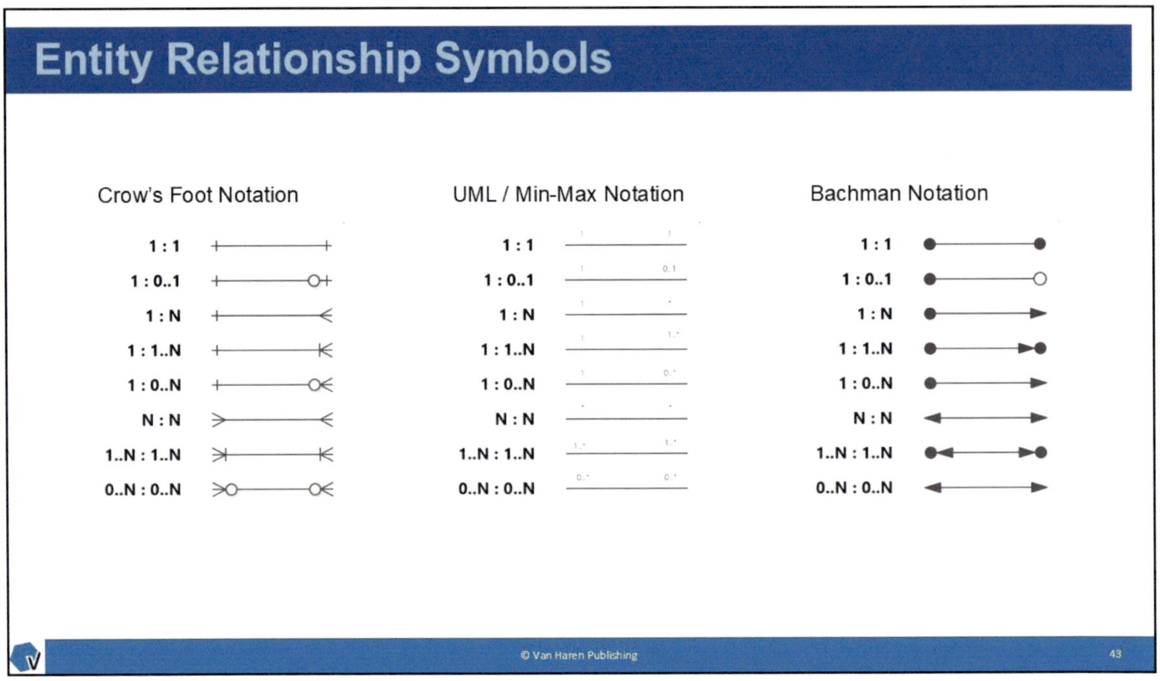
Entity Relationship Symbols
Crow's Foot Notation
1 : 1
1 : 0..1
1 : N
1 : 1..N
1 : 0..N
N : N
1..N : 1..N
0..N : 0..N
UML / Min-Max Notation
1 : 1
1 : 0..1
1 : N
1 : 1..N
1 : 0..N
N : N
1..N : 1..N
0..N : 0..N
Bachman Notation
1 : 1
1 : 0..1
1 : N
1 : 1..N
1 : 0..N
N : N
1..N : 1..N
0..N : 0..N
© Van Haren Publishing
43

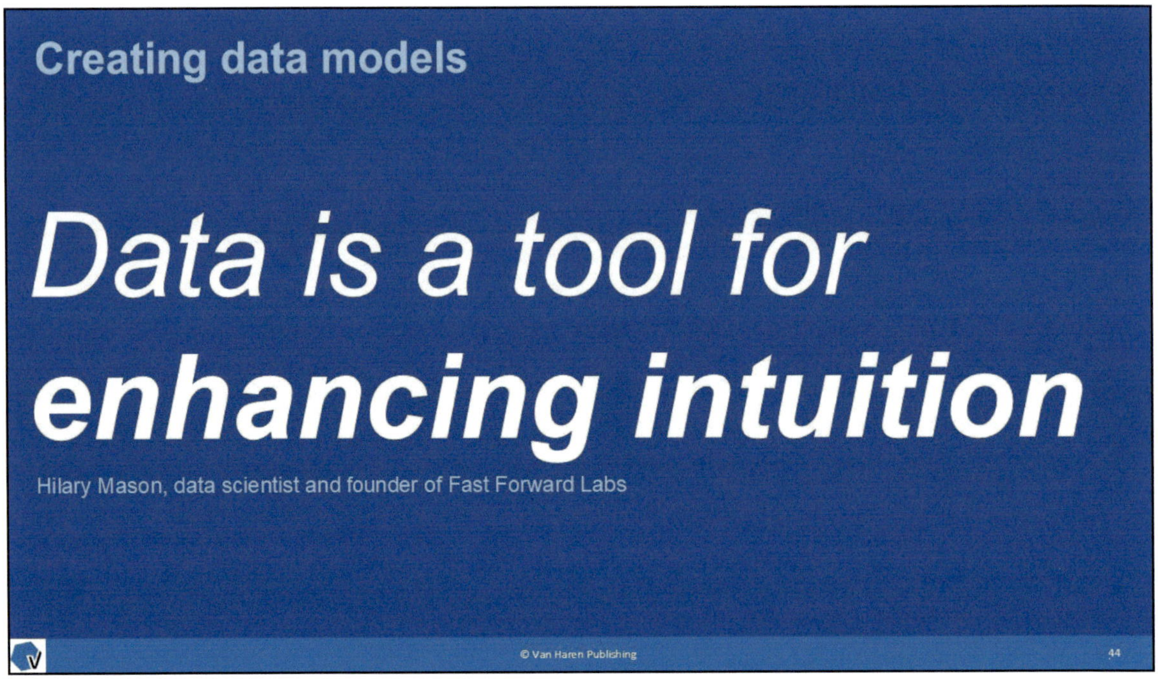
Creating data models
Data is a tool for
enhancing intuition
Hilary Mason, data scientist and founder of Fast Forward Labs
© Van Haren Publishing
44

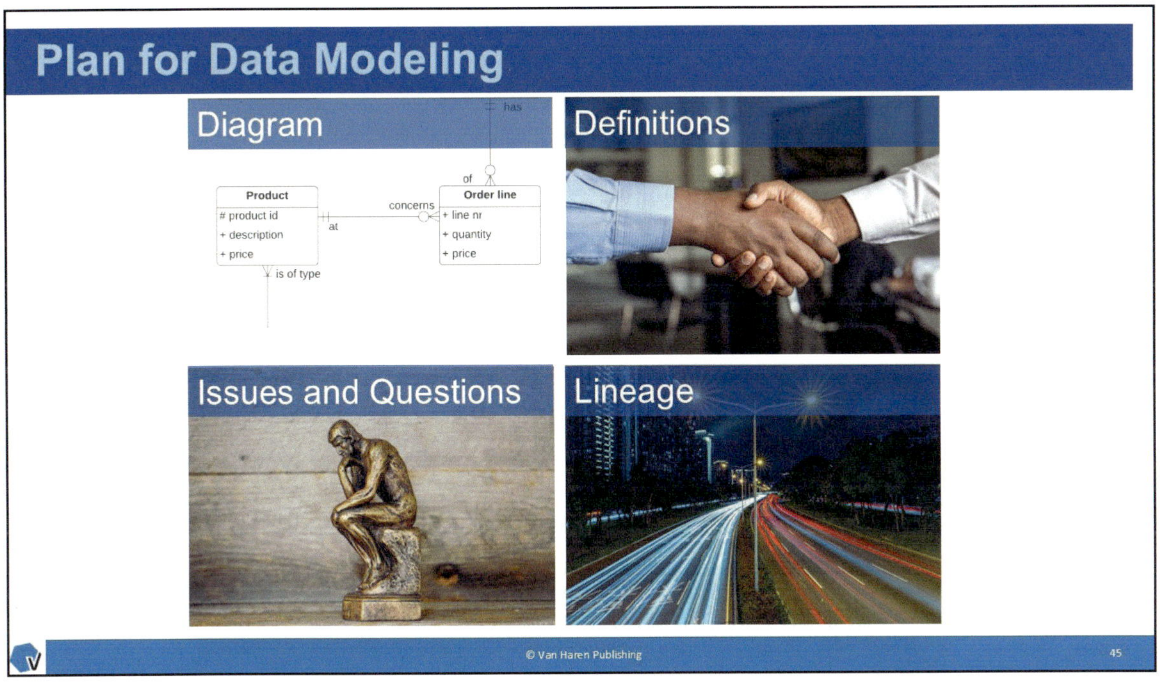

Exercise: Conceptual Data Model

Artist	A person, or group of persons, who creates, performs or produces music as a profession.
Music Track	A recorded piece of music with melody, rhythm, and instruments.
Consumer	A person who engages with and experiences the auditory and emotional aspect of musical compositions, either by actively choosing to hear them or by passively encountering them. This person has an active *subscription* to a *music platform*.
Playback	The event in which a *Music Track* is played by a *Consumer* on a *Platform*.
Platform	A software service on which *Music Tracks* are hosted and that allows for the playback of *Music Tracks*.

 46

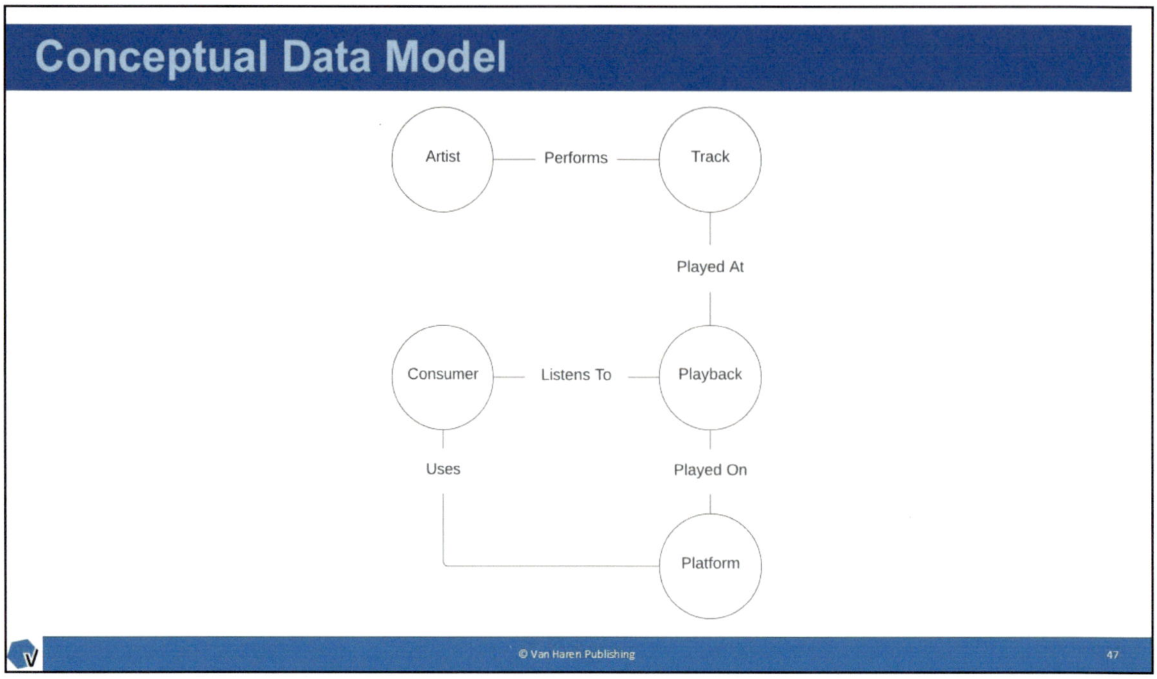
Conceptual Data Model
Artist
Performs
Track
Played At
Consumer
Listens To
Playback
Uses
Played On
Platform
© Van Haren Publishing
47

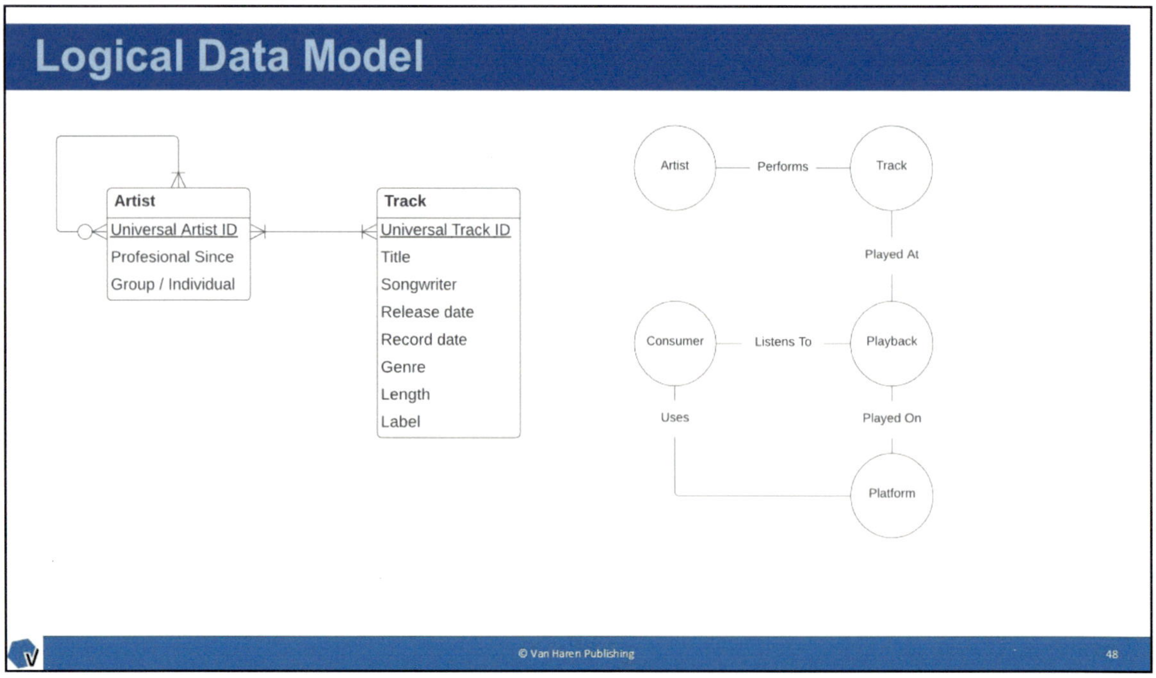
Logical Data Model
Artist
Universal Artist ID
Profesional Since
Group / Individual
Track
Universal Track ID
Title
Songwriter
Release date
Record date
Genre
Length
Label
Artist
Performs
Track
Played At
Consumer
Listens To
Playback
Uses
Played On
Platform
© Van Haren Publishing
48

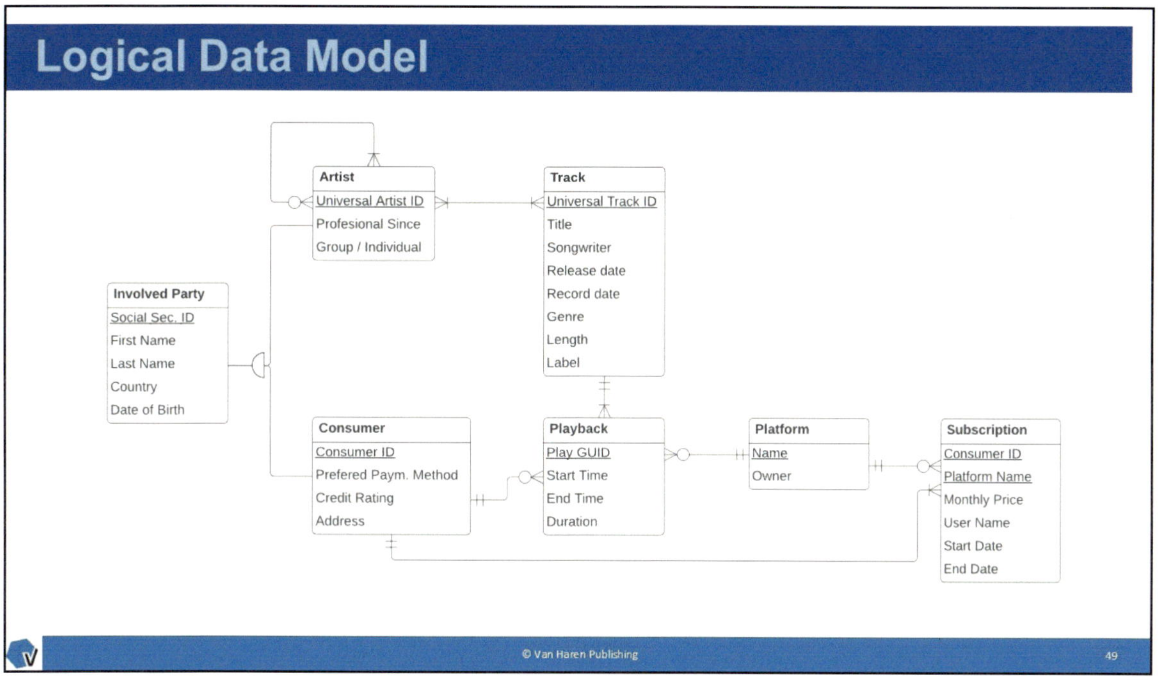
Logical Data Model
Artist
Universal Artist ID
Profesional Since
Group / Individual
Track
Universal Track ID
Title
Songwriter
Release date
Record date
Genre
Length
Label
Involved Party
Social Sec. ID
First Name
Last Name
Country
Date of Birth
Consumer
Consumer ID
Prefered Paym. Method
Credit Rating
Address
Playback
Play GUID
Start Time
End Time
Duration
Platform
Name
Owner
Subscription
Consumer ID
Platform Name
Monthly Price
User Name
Start Date
End Date
© Van Haren Publishing
49

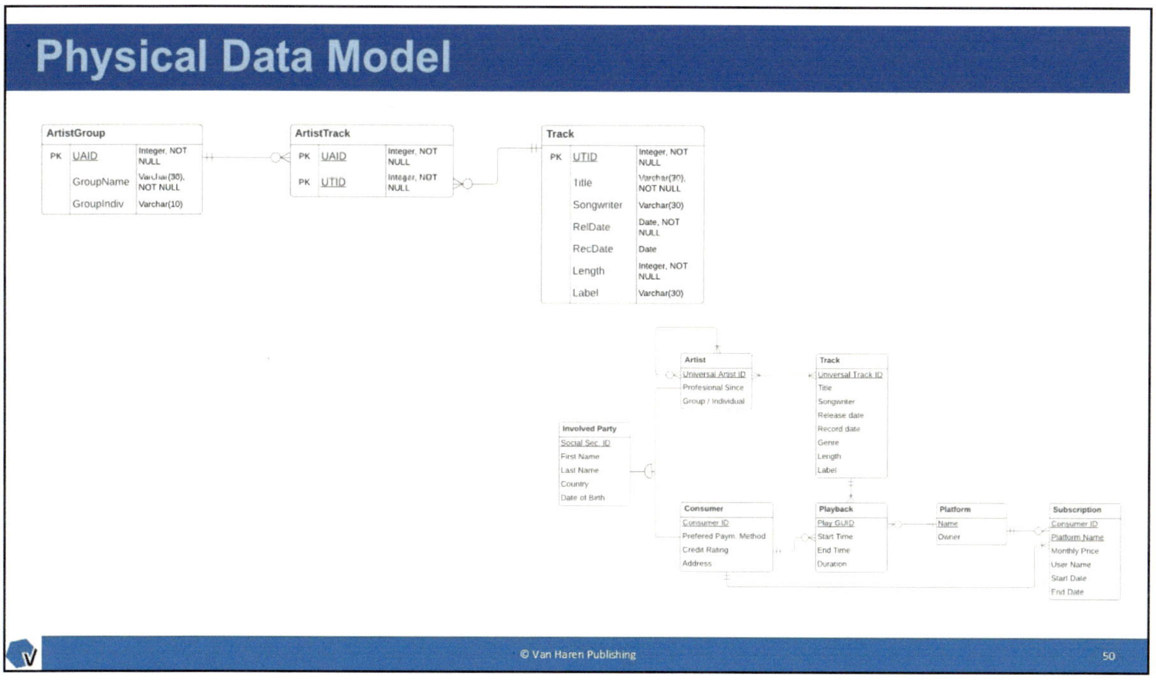
Physical Data Model
ArtistGroup
PK UAID Integer, NOT NULL
GroupName Varchar(30), NOT NULL
GroupIndiv Varchar(10)
ArtistTrack
PK UAID Integer, NOT NULL
PK UTID Integer, NOT NULL
Track
PK UTID Integer, NOT NULL
Title Varchar(30), NOT NULL
Songwriter Varchar(30)
RelDate Date, NOT NULL
RecDate Date
Length Integer, NOT NULL
Label Varchar(30)
© Van Haren Publishing
50

Physical Data Model

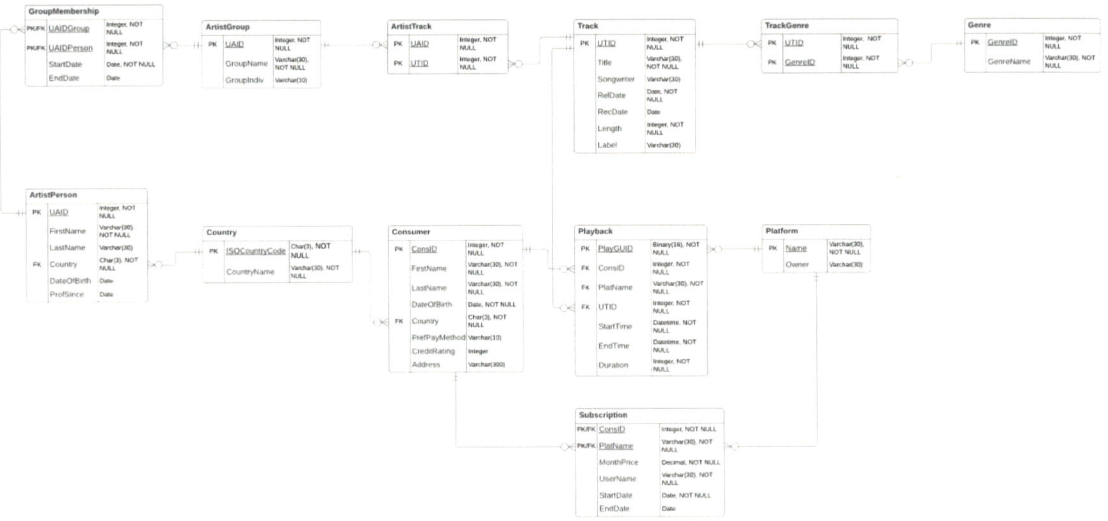

 51

Review Data Models

The Data Modeling Scorecard

#	Category	Total Score	Model Score	%	Comments
1	How well does the model capture the requirements?	15			
2	How complete is the model?	15			
3	How well does the model match its scheme?	10			
4	How structurally sound is the model?	15			
5	How well does the model leverage generic structures	10			
6	How well does the model follow naming standards?	5			
7	How well has the model been arranged for readability?	5			
8	How good are the definitions	10			
9	How consistent is the model with the enterprise	5			
10	How wel does the metadata match the data?	10			
	TOTAL SCORE	100			

 52

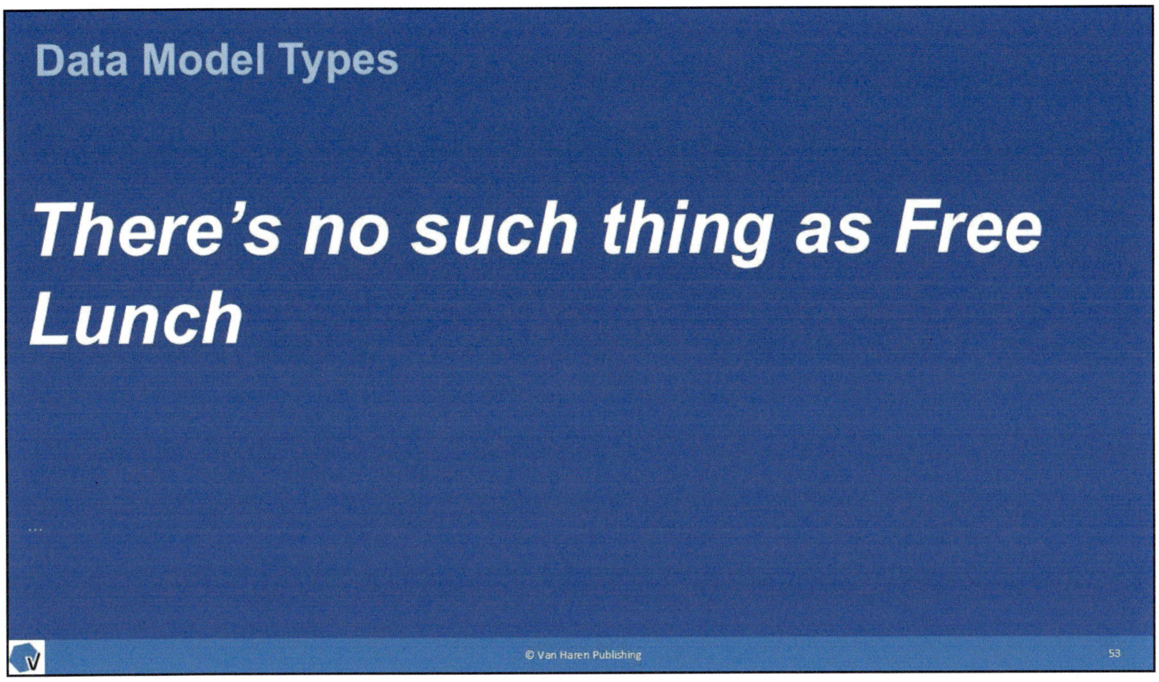
Data Model Types
There's no such thing as Free Lunch
...
© Van Haren Publishing
53

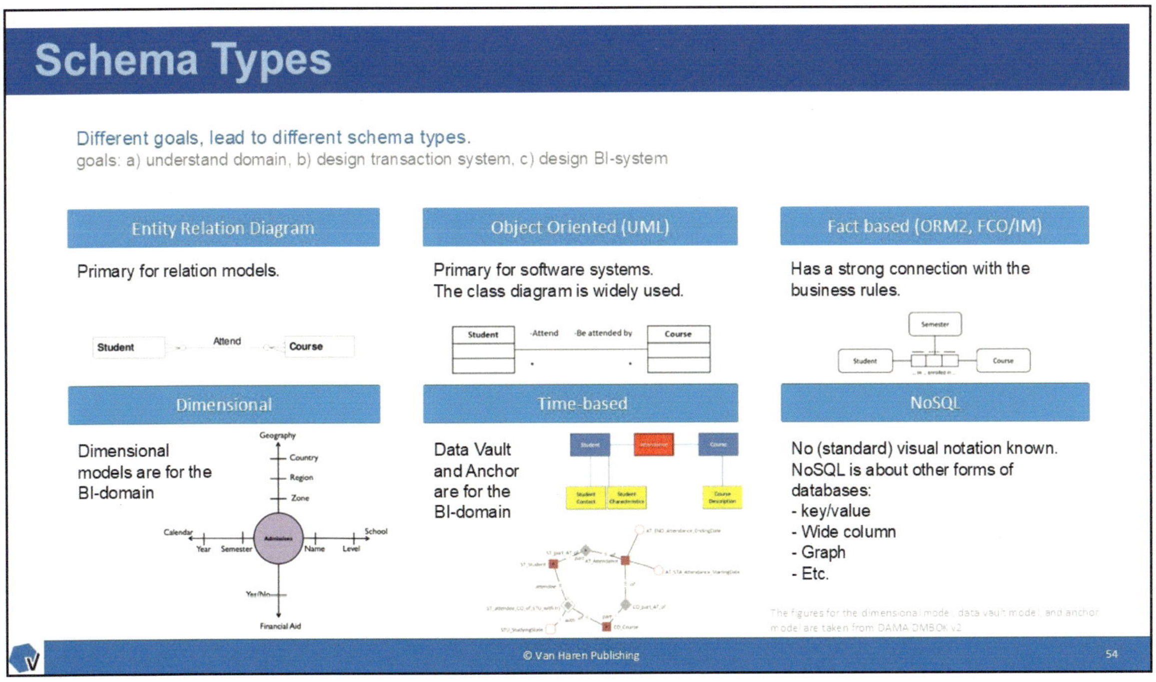
Schema Types
Different goals, lead to different schema types.
goals: a) understand domain, b) design transaction system, c) design BI-system
Entity Relation Diagram
Primary for relation models.
Student
Attend
Course
Object Oriented (UML)
Primary for software systems.
The class diagram is widely used.
Student
Attend
Be attended by
Course
Fact based (ORM2, FCO/IM)
Has a strong connection with the business rules.
Semester
Student
Course
Dimensional
Dimensional models are for the BI-domain
Geography
Country
Region
Zone
Calendar
Year
Semester
Admissions
Name
Level
School
Yes/No
Financial Aid
Time-based
Data Vault and Anchor are for the BI-domain
NoSQL
No (standard) visual notation known.
NoSQL is about other forms of databases:
- key/value
- Wide column
- Graph
- Etc.
The figures for the dimensional model, data vault model, and anchor model are taken from DAMA DMBOK v2
© Van Haren Publishing
54

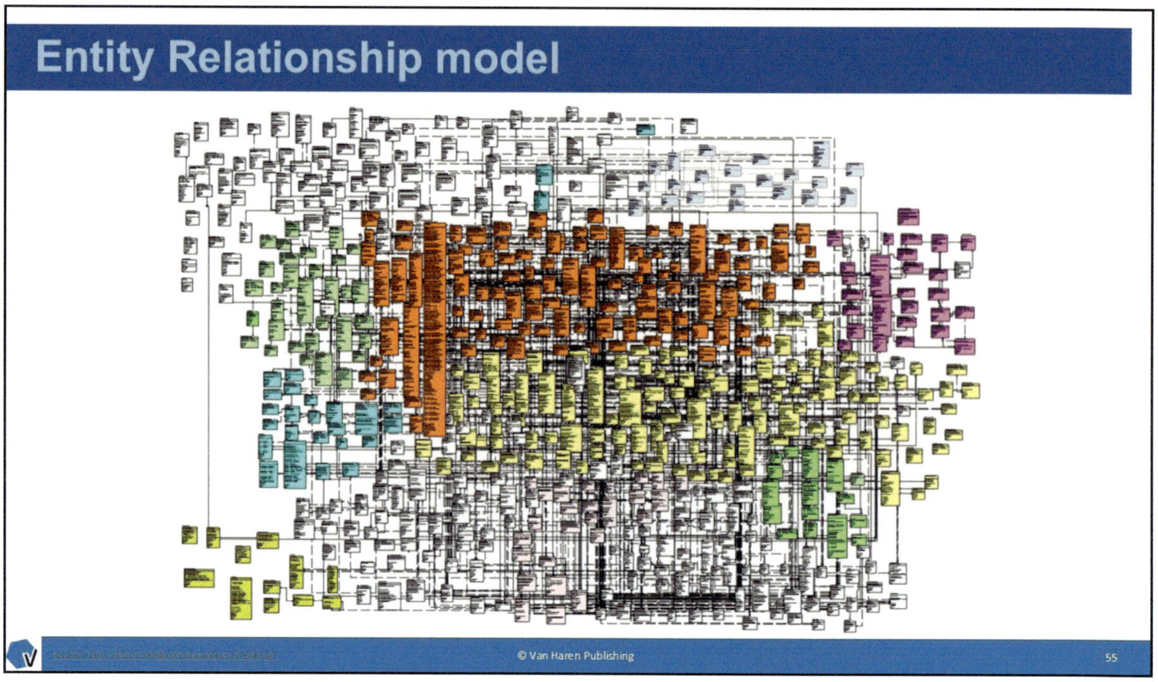
Entity Relationship model
© Van Haren Publishing
55

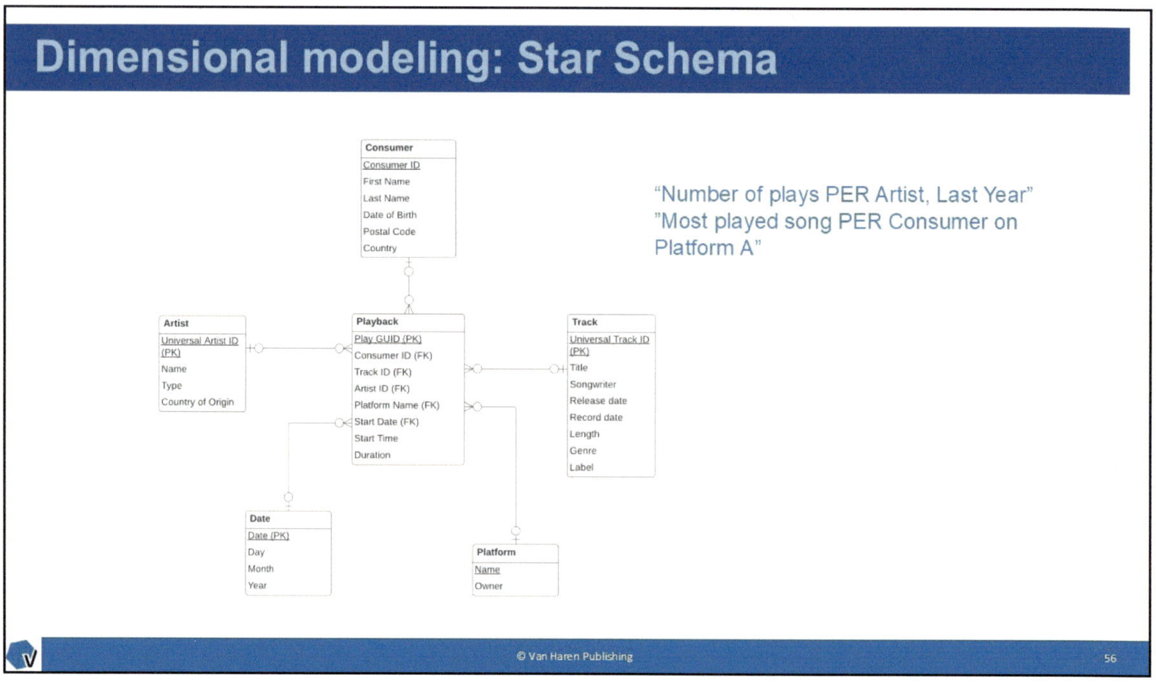
Dimensional modeling: Star Schema
Consumer
Consumer ID
First Name
Last Name
Date of Birth
Postal Code
Country
"Number of plays PER Artist, Last Year"
"Most played song PER Consumer on Platform A"
Artist
Universal Artist ID (PK)
Name
Type
Country of Origin
Playback
Play GUID (PK)
Consumer ID (FK)
Track ID (FK)
Artist ID (FK)
Platform Name (FK)
Start Date (FK)
Start Time
Duration
Track
Universal Track ID (PK)
Title
Songwriter
Release date
Record date
Length
Genre
Label
Date
Date (PK)
Day
Month
Year
Platform
Name
Owner
© Van Haren Publishing
56

Slowly Changing Dimensions

Player

Player ID	Name	Club	Country
1001	H. Kane	Tottenham Hotspur	UK

Goals

Player ID	Season	Goals
...	...	...
1001	2020-2021	33
1001	2021-2022	27
1001	2022-2023	32

"Player H. Kane scored 280 goals for Tottenham Hotspur"

Player

Player ID	Name	Club	Country
1001	H. Kane	Bayern Munich	GER

Goals

Player ID	Season	Goals
...	...	...
1001	2020-2021	33
1001	2021-2022	27
1001	2022-2023	32

"Player H. Kane scored 280 goals for Bayern Munich"

 57

Slowly Changing Dimensions

Player

Player ID	Name	Club	Country
1001	H. Kane	Tottenham Hotspur	UK

Type 1: Overwrite

Player

Player ID	Name	Club	Country
1001	H. Kane	Bayern Munich	GER

Type 2: New Row

Player

Player ID	Name	Club	Version
1001	H. Kane	Tottenham Hotspur	0
1001	H. Kane	Bayern Munich	1

Player

Player ID	Name	Club	Start Date	End Date
1001	H. Kane	Tottenham Hotspur	2009-10-09	2023-08-10
1001	H. Kane	Bayern Munich	2023-08-11	NULL

 58

Slowly Changing Dimensions

Player

Player ID	Name	Club	Country
1001	H. Kane	Tottenham Hotspur	UK

Type 3: New Column

Player

Player ID	Name	Original Club	Current Club
1001	H. Kane	Tottenham Hotspur	Bayern Munich

Type 4: History Table

Player

Player ID	Name	Club
1001	H. Kane	Bayern Munich

Player History

Player ID	Name	Club	Date Created
1001	H. Kane	Tottenham Hotspur	2009-10-09
1001	H. Kane	Bayern Munich	2023-08-11

59

Grain

Fact Tables

Transaction Fact Table

A customer does a thing, and you record a transaction in your data warehouse

Periodic Snapshot Table

For every period, you record how often a certain event occurred

Accumulating Snapshot Table

A customer does a series of things, and you record a measurement for each step along the process

Factless Fact Table

A customer does a thing on a date, and you record the dimensions only

 61

Conformed Facts & Conformed Dimensions

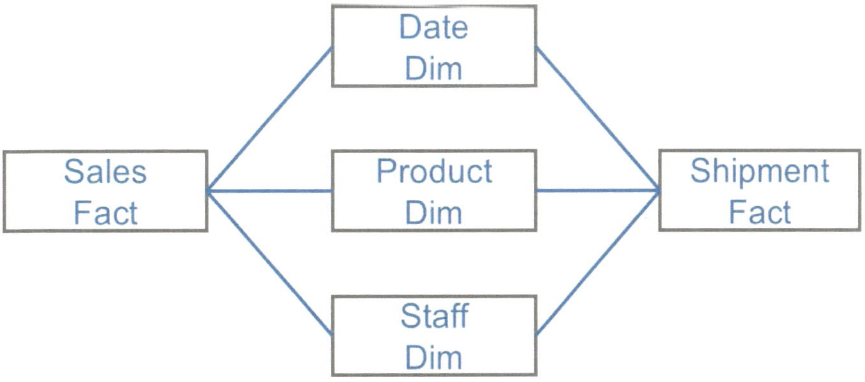

 62

Conformed Dimensions – Bus Matrix

Process \ Dimension	Date	Customer	Product	Sales Organization	Service Line	Warehouse	Rate Plan	Switch	Support Call Profile	Employee	Location
Purchasing	x		x			x				x	x
Internal Inventory	x		x			x					x
Channel Inventory	x		x	x							x
Service Activation	x	x	x	x	x		x				x
Product Sales	x	x	x	x	x		x				x
Promotion Participation	x	x	x	x	x		x				
Call Detail Traffic	x	x	x	x	x		x	x			
Customer Billing	x	x	x	x	x		x				x
Customer Support Calls	x	x	x	x	x		x		x	x	
Repair Work Orders	x	x	x		x				x	x	
Payments from Customer	x	x			x				x		
Returns	x	x	x	x	x				x	x	x

© Van Haren Publishing 63

Dimensional: Snowflaking

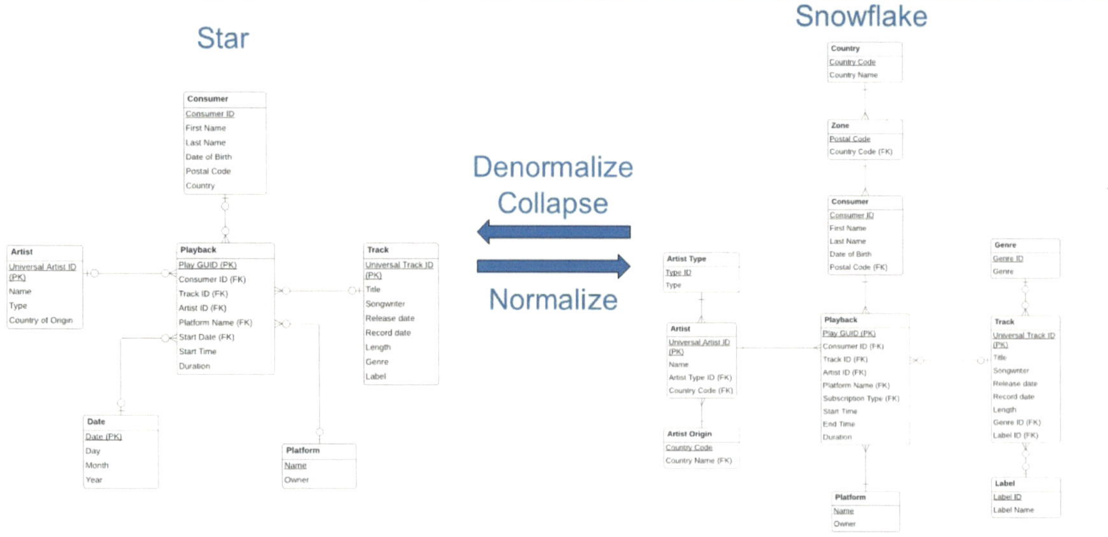

© Van Haren Publishing 64

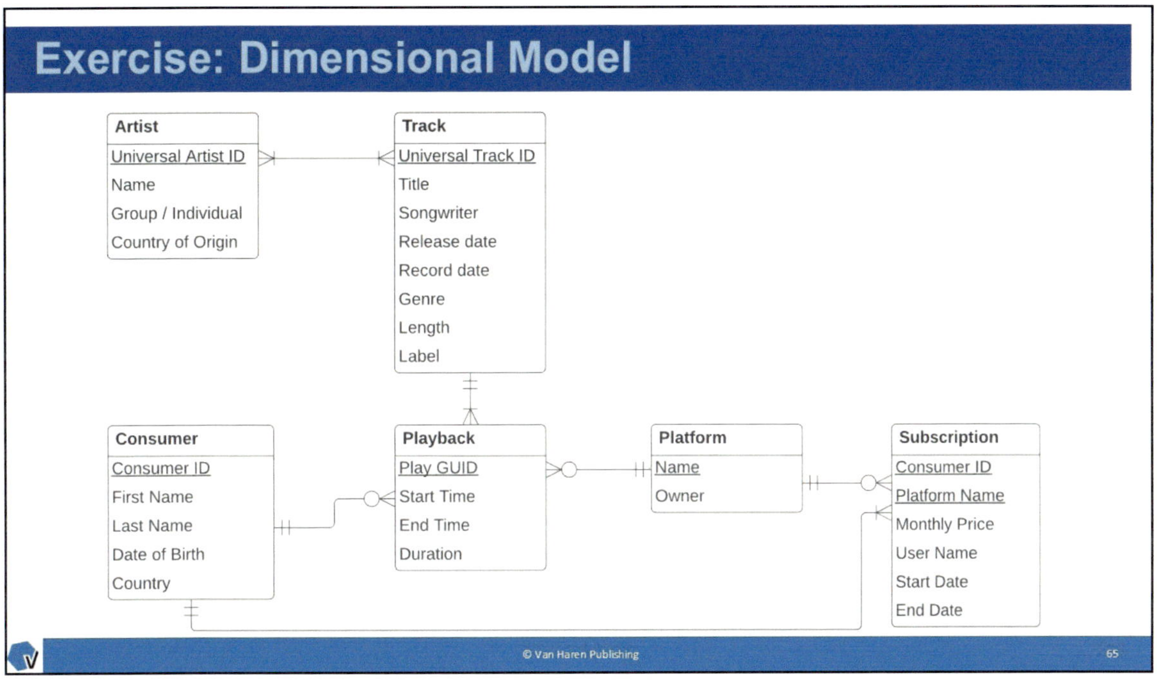
Exercise: Dimensional Model
Artist
Universal Artist ID
Name
Group / Individual
Country of Origin
Track
Universal Track ID
Title
Songwriter
Release date
Record date
Genre
Length
Label
Consumer
Consumer ID
First Name
Last Name
Date of Birth
Country
Playback
Play GUID
Start Time
End Time
Duration
Platform
Name
Owner
Subscription
Consumer ID
Platform Name
Monthly Price
User Name
Start Date
End Date
© Van Haren Publishing
65

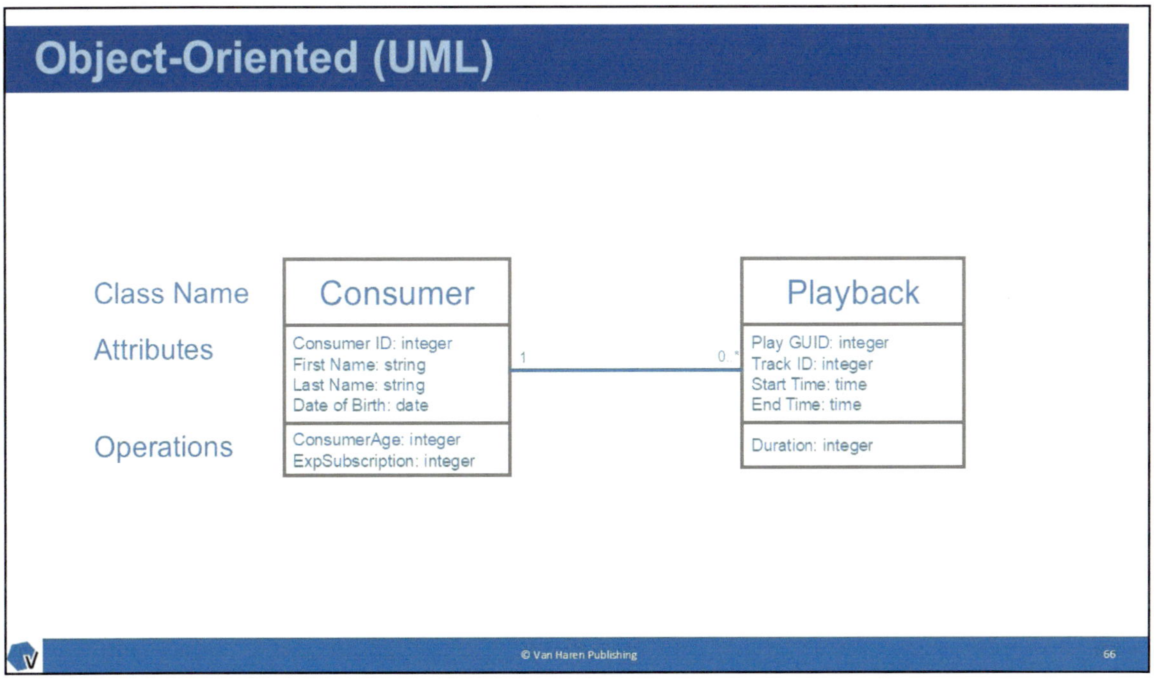
Object-Oriented (UML)
Class Name
Attributes
Operations
Consumer
Consumer ID: integer
First Name: string
Last Name: string
Date of Birth: date
ConsumerAge: integer
ExpSubscription: integer
1
Playback
Play GUID: integer
Track ID: integer
Start Time: time
End Time: time
Duration: integer
© Van Haren Publishing
66

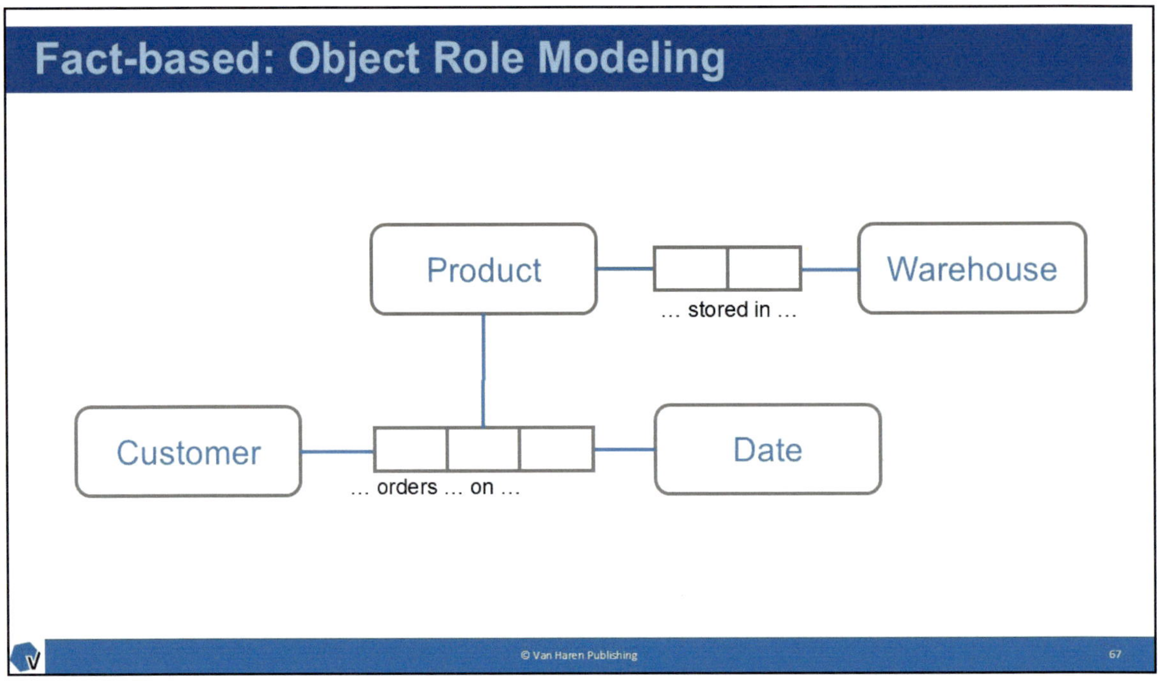
Fact-based: Object Role Modeling
Product
... stored in ...
Warehouse
Customer
... orders ... on ...
Date
© Van Haren Publishing
67

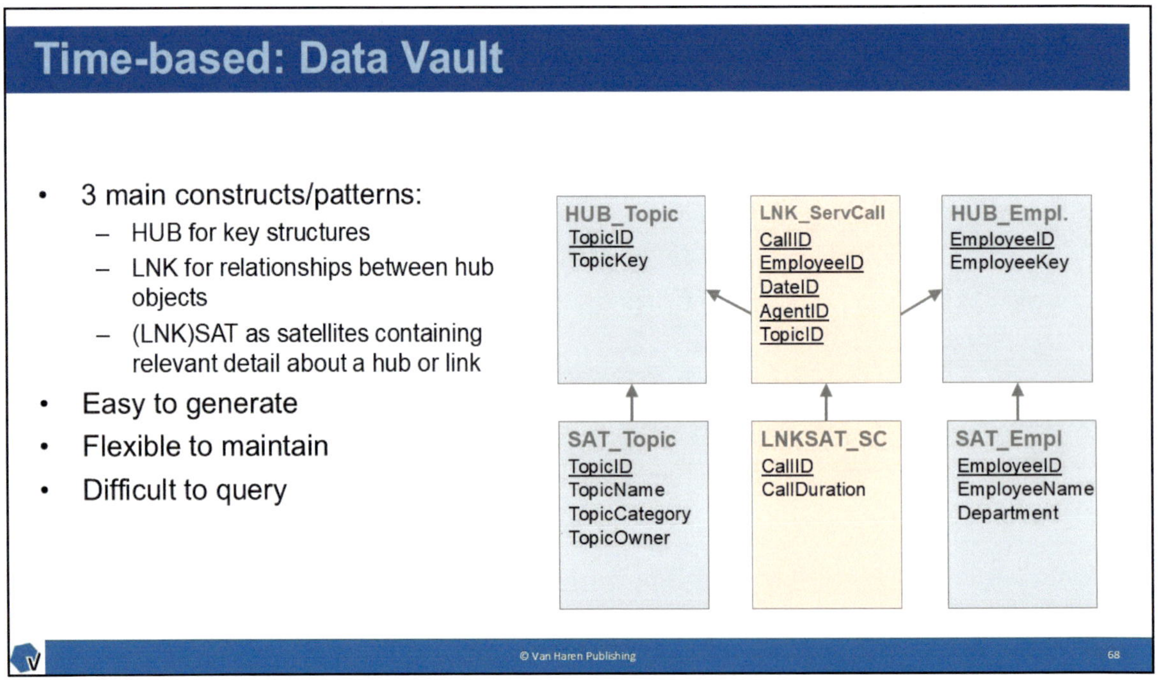
Time-based: Data Vault
• 3 main constructs/patterns:
– HUB for key structures
– LNK for relationships between hub objects
– (LNK)SAT as satellites containing relevant detail about a hub or link
• Easy to generate
• Flexible to maintain
• Difficult to query
HUB_Topic
TopicID
TopicKey
LNK_ServCall
CallID
EmployeeID
DateID
AgentID
TopicID
HUB_Empl.
EmployeeID
EmployeeKey
SAT_Topic
TopicID
TopicName
TopicCategory
TopicOwner
LNKSAT_SC
CallID
CallDuration
SAT_Empl
EmployeeID
EmployeeName
Department
© Van Haren Publishing
68

Time-based: Anchor Modeling

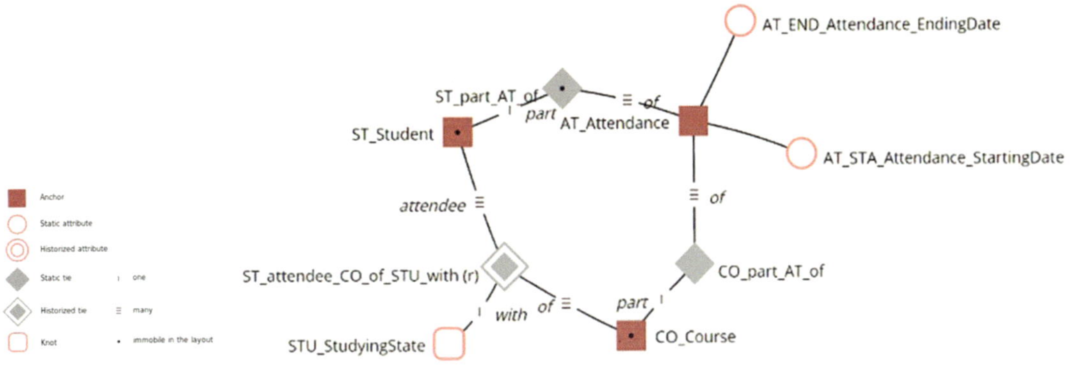

 69

NoSQL

Document
- Data stored as self-contained docs
- Different structure per document
- Often XML, YAML, and JSON

Key-value
- Data stored as key-value pairs
- Fast read and write operations

Column-oriented
- Data stored in columns
- Supports complex data types
- Good for time-series data, analytical workloads and horizontal scalability

Graph
- Data represents nodes, edges and properties
- Graph traversing
- Social networks and recommendation systems

 70

Normalization

The process of structuring a relational database in order to ***reduce data redundancy*** *and* ***improve data integrity***

Why Normalization?

To free the collection of relations from **undesirable insertion, update and deletion dependencies**.

Insert

Artist	Song	Website
The Beatles	Come Together	TheBeatles.com
The Beatles	Let It Be	TheBeatles.com
The Rolling Stones	Paint It, Black	RollingStones.com

AC/DC	TNT	???

Update

Artist	Song	Website
The Beatles	Come Together	TheBeatles.com
The Beatles	Let It Be	TheBeatles.com
The Rolling Stones	Paint It, Black	RollingStones.com

Artist	Song	Website
The Beatles	Come Together	TheBeatles.com
The Beatles	Let It Be	Beatles.com
The Rolling Stones	Paint It, Black	RollingStones.com

Delete

Artist	Song	Website
The Beatles	Come Together	TheBeatles.com
The Beatles	Let It Be	TheBeatles.com
The Rolling Stones	Paint It, Black	RollingStones.com

Artist	Song	Website
The Beatles	Come Together	TheBeatles.com
The Beatles	Let It Be	TheBeatles.com
The Rolling Stones	~~Paint It, Black~~	RollingStones.com

Normalization

First Normal Form (1NF, 1970)

- Table columns must contain atomic values.
- The table must not have any repeating groups.
- Every row in the table must be identifiable by a primary key.

Artist	Song
The Beatles	Come Together (1969) Penny Lane (1967) Let It Be (1970) A Day In The Life (1967)
The Rolling Stones	Paint It, Black (1966) Start Me Up (1981) Satisfaction (1965)

 73

Normalization

First Normal Form (1NF, 1970)

- Table columns must contain atomic values.
- The table must not have any repeating groups.
- Every row in the table must be identifiable by a primary key.

Artist	Song
The Beatles	Come Together (1969) Penny Lane (1967) Let It Be (1970) A Day In The Life (1967)
The Rolling Stones	Paint It, Black (1966) Start Me Up (1981) Satisfaction (1965)

Artist	Song	Release Year
The Beatles	Come Together	1969
The Beatles	Penny Lane	1967
The Beatles	Let It Be	1970
The Beatles	A Day In The Life	1967
The Rolling Stones	Paint It, Black	1966
The Rolling Stones	Start Me Up	1981
The Rolling Stones	Satisfaction	1965

Artist	Song_1	Release Year 1	Song 2	Release Year 2	Song 3	Release Year 3	Song 4	Release Year 4
The Beatles	Come Together	1969	Penny Lane	1967	Let It Be	1970	A Day In The Life	1967
The Rolling Stones	Paint It, Black	1966	Start Me Up	1981	Satisfaction	1965		

 74

Normalization

Second Normal Form (2NF, 1971)

Every non-prime attribute is functionally dependent on a candidate key (every non-prime attribute depend on the whole of every key)

Artist	Song	Release Year	Website
The Beatles	Come Together	1969	TheBeatles.com
The Beatles	Penny Lane	1967	TheBeatles.com
The Beatles	Let It Be	1970	TheBeatles.com
The Beatles	A Day In The Life	1967	TheBeatles.com
The Rolling Stones	Paint It, Black	1966	RollingStones.com
The Rolling Stones	Start Me Up	1981	RollingStones.com
The Rolling Stones	Satisfaction	1965	RollingStones.com

Candidate key: {Artist, Song}
Non-prime attributes: Release Year, Website

{Artist, Song} → {Release Year}
{Artist} → {Website}

 75

Normalization

Second Normal Form (2NF, 1971)

Every non-prime attribute is functionally dependent on a candidate key (every non-prime attribute depend on the whole of every key)

Artist	Song	Release Year
The Beatles	Come Together	1969
The Beatles	Penny Lane	1967
The Beatles	Let It Be	1970
The Beatles	A Day In The Life	1967
The Rolling Stones	Paint It, Black	1966
The Rolling Stones	Start Me Up	1981
The Rolling Stones	Satisfaction	1965

Artist	Website
The Beatles	TheBeatles.com
The Rolling Stones	RollingStones.com

 76

Normalization

Third Normal Form (3NF, 1971)

All non-prime attributes depend only on the candidate keys and do not have a transitive dependency on another key.

"Every non-key attribute depends on the key, the whole key and nothing but the key"

Artist	Song	Release Year	Rating Score	Rating
The Beatles	Come Together	1969	8	Great
The Beatles	Penny Lane	1967	9	Great
The Beatles	Let It Be	1970	7	Good
The Beatles	A Day In The Life	1967	10	Amazing
The Rolling Stones	Paint It, Black	1966	8	Great
The Rolling Stones	Start Me Up	1981	6	Good
The Rolling Stones	Satisfaction	1965	10	Amazing

{Artist, Song} → {Rating Score}

{Artist, Song} → {Rating Score} → {Rating}

© Van Haren Publishing 77

Normalization

Third Normal Form (3NF, 1971)

All non-prime attributes depend only on the candidate keys and do not have a transitive dependency on another key.

"Every non-key attribute depends on the key, the whole key and nothing but the key"

Artist	Song	Release Year	Rating Score
The Beatles	Come Together	1969	8
The Beatles	Penny Lane	1967	9
The Beatles	Let It Be	1970	7
The Beatles	A Day In The Life	1967	10
The Rolling Stones	Paint It, Black	1966	8
The Rolling Stones	Start Me Up	1981	6
The Rolling Stones	Satisfaction	1965	10

Rating Score	Rating
1	Poor
2	Poor
3	Poor
4	Fair
5	Fair
6	Good
7	Good
8	Great
9	Great
10	Amazing

© Van Haren Publishing 78

Normalization

Release_ Year	Album	Release_ Year_and _Month	Ranking
1969	Abbey Road	1969-09	1
1969	Led Zeppelin II	1969-10	2
1969	Tommy	1969-05	3
1974	On the Beach	1974-07	1
1974	Country Life	1974-11	2
1974	Sheer Heart Attack	1974-11	3

Candidate Keys

{Album}
{Release_Year, Ranking}
{Release_Year_and_Month, Ranking}

Prime Attributes

Every attribute is a prime attribute, there are no non-prime attributes

Normal Form

3NF: "Each non-prime attribute depends on the key, the whole key and nothing but the key"

 79

Normalization

Boyce-Codd Normal Form (BCNF, 1974)

Every ~~non-key~~ attribute in a table should depend on the key, the whole key and nothing but the key (where key = "every candidate key")

Release_ Year	Album	Release_ Year_and_ Month	Ranking
1969	Abbey Road	1969-09	1
1969	Led Zeppelin II	1969-10	2
1969	Tommy	1969-05	3
1974	On the Beach	1974-07	1
1974	Country Life	1974-11	2
1974	Sheer Heart Attack	1974-11	3

 80

Normalization

Boyce-Codd Normal Form (BCNF, 1974)

Every ~~non-key~~ attribute in a table should depend on the key, the whole key and nothing but the key (where key = "every candidate key")

Release_ Year	Album	Release_ Month	Ranking
1969	Abbey Road	September	1
1969	Led Zeppelin II	October	2
1969	Tommy	May	3
1974	On the Beach	July	1
1974	Country Life	November	2
1974	Sheer Heart Attack	November	3

 81

Normalization

Fourth Normal Form (4NF, 1977)

Every non-trivial multivalued dependency begins with a superkey
"Multivalued dependencies in a table must be multivalued dependencies on the key"

<u>Platform</u>	<u>Song</u>	<u>Subscription</u>
Spotify	Come Together	Normal
Spotify	Come Together	Family
Spotify	Penny Lane	Normal
Spotify	Penny Lane	Family
Apple Music	Come Together	Normal
Apple Music	Come Together	Family
Apple Music	Let It Be	Normal
Apple Music	Let It Be	Family

Satisfies BCNF: Table has no non-prime attributes because the only candidate key is {Platform, Song, Subscription}

However:

- IF we assume all songs are available on all subscriptions, then the table features two non-trivial dependencies on the {Platform} attribute (which is not a superkey):

$\{Platform\} \twoheadrightarrow \{Song\}$
$\{Platform\} \twoheadrightarrow \{Subscription\}$

Risk of anomalies!

 82

Normalization

Fourth Normal Form (4NF, 1977)

Every non-trivial multivalued dependency begins with a superkey

Platform	Song	Subscription
Spotify	Come Together	Normal
Spotify	Come Together	Family
Spotify	Penny Lane	Normal
Spotify	Penny Lane	Family
Apple Music	Come Together	Normal
Apple Music	Come Together	Family
Apple Music	Let It Be	Normal
Apple Music	Let It Be	Family

Platform	Song
Spotify	Come Together
Spotify	Penny Lane
Apple Music	Come Together
Apple Music	Let It Be

Platform	Subscription
Spotify	Normal
Spotify	Family
Apple Music	Normal
Apple Music	Family

In contrast: if the availability of a song IS dependent on the subscription, then the original table would satisfy 4NF

 83

Denormalization

 84

Design Principles & Best Practices

Everything is designed.
Few things are designed well.

Brian Reed, front-end developer and musician

Database Design Principles

Database Design Best Practices

Denormalization / Normalization
Normalize or Denormalize your data, depending on (a.o.) read or write optimization.

Surrogate keys
Substitute keys not visible to the business.

Indexing
Create index files to improve query performance.

Views
Control access to data elements, or embed common join conditions or filters.

Partitioning
Break a table horizontally or vertically, to improve scalability, reduce contention and optimize performance.

 87

Partitioning

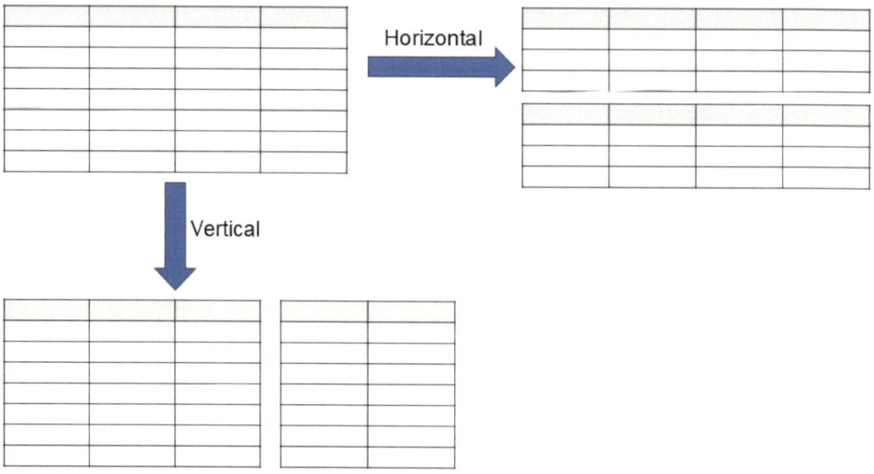

 88

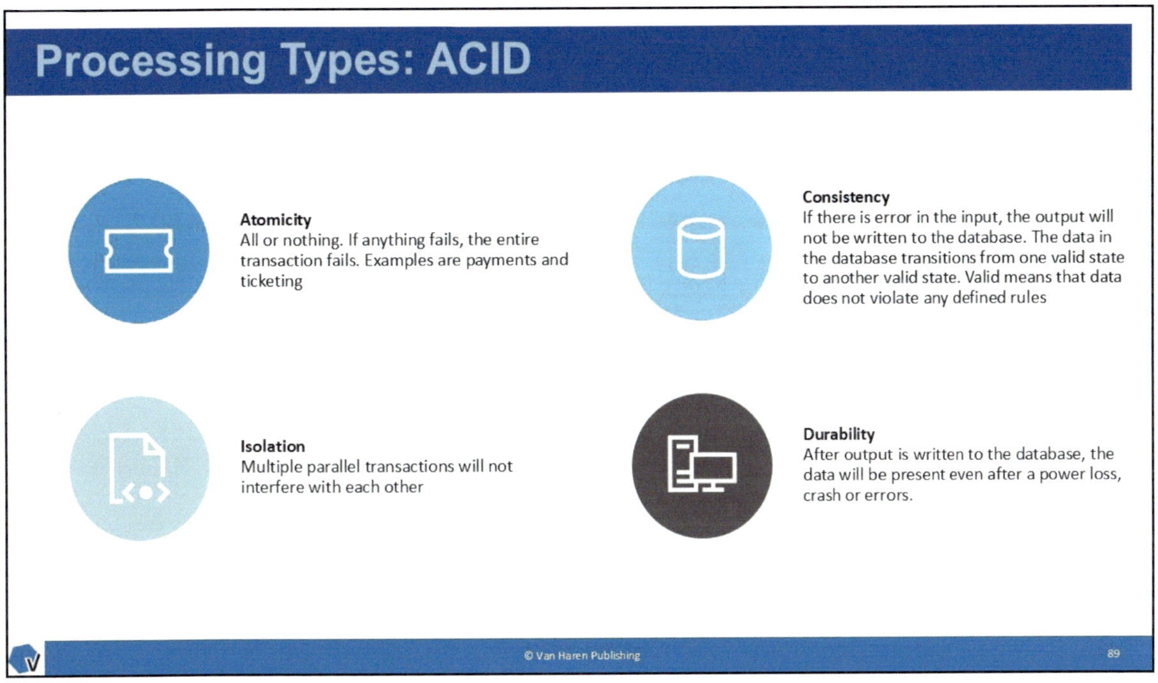
Processing Types: ACID
Atomicity
All or nothing. If anything fails, the entire transaction fails. Examples are payments and ticketing
Consistency
If there is error in the input, the output will not be written to the database. The data in the database transitions from one valid state to another valid state. Valid means that data does not violate any defined rules
Isolation
Multiple parallel transactions will not interfere with each other
Durability
After output is written to the database, the data will be present even after a power loss, crash or errors.
© Van Haren Publishing
89

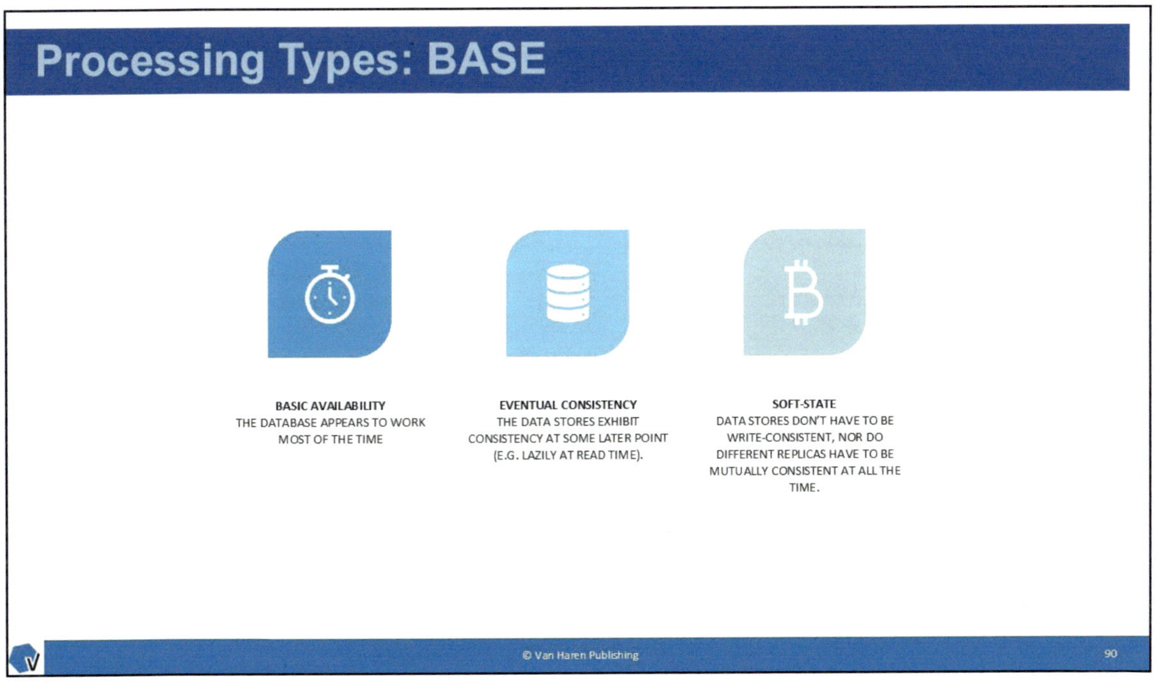
Processing Types: BASE
BASIC AVAILABILITY
THE DATABASE APPEARS TO WORK MOST OF THE TIME
EVENTUAL CONSISTENCY
THE DATA STORES EXHIBIT CONSISTENCY AT SOME LATER POINT (E.G. LAZILY AT READ TIME).
SOFT-STATE
DATA STORES DON'T HAVE TO BE WRITE-CONSISTENT, NOR DO DIFFERENT REPLICAS HAVE TO BE MUTUALLY CONSISTENT AT ALL THE TIME.
© Van Haren Publishing
90

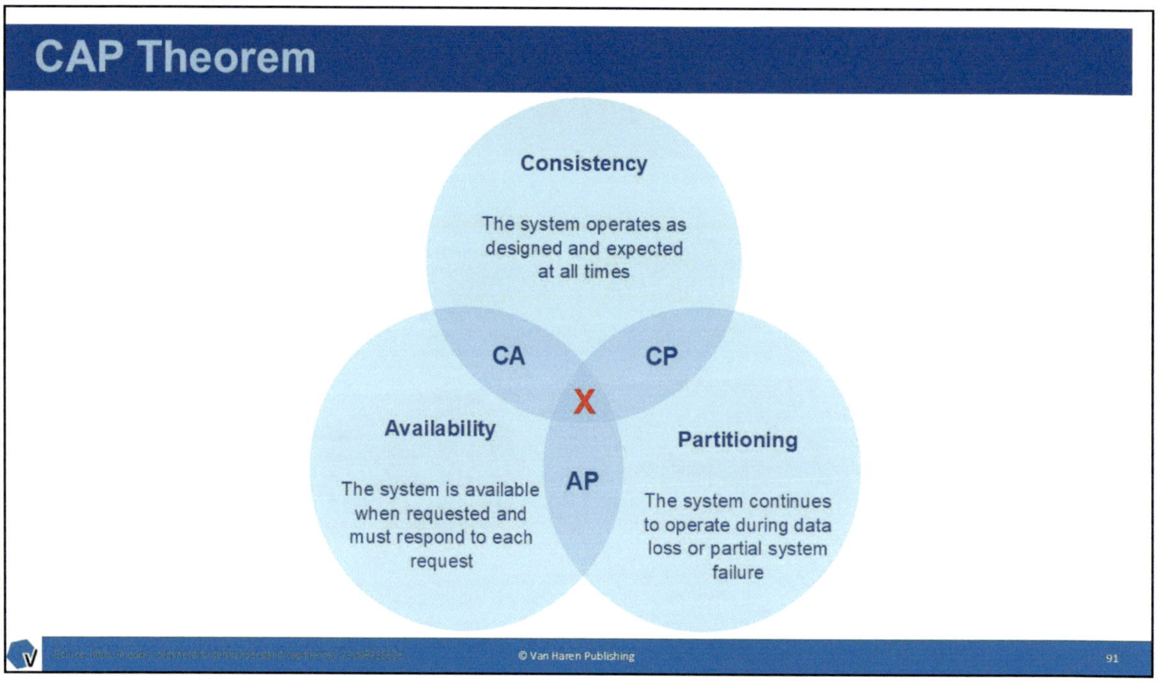
CAP Theorem
Consistency
The system operates as designed and expected at all times
CA
CP
X
Availability
The system is available when requested and must respond to each request
AP
Partitioning
The system continues to operate during data loss or partial system failure
© Van Haren Publishing
91

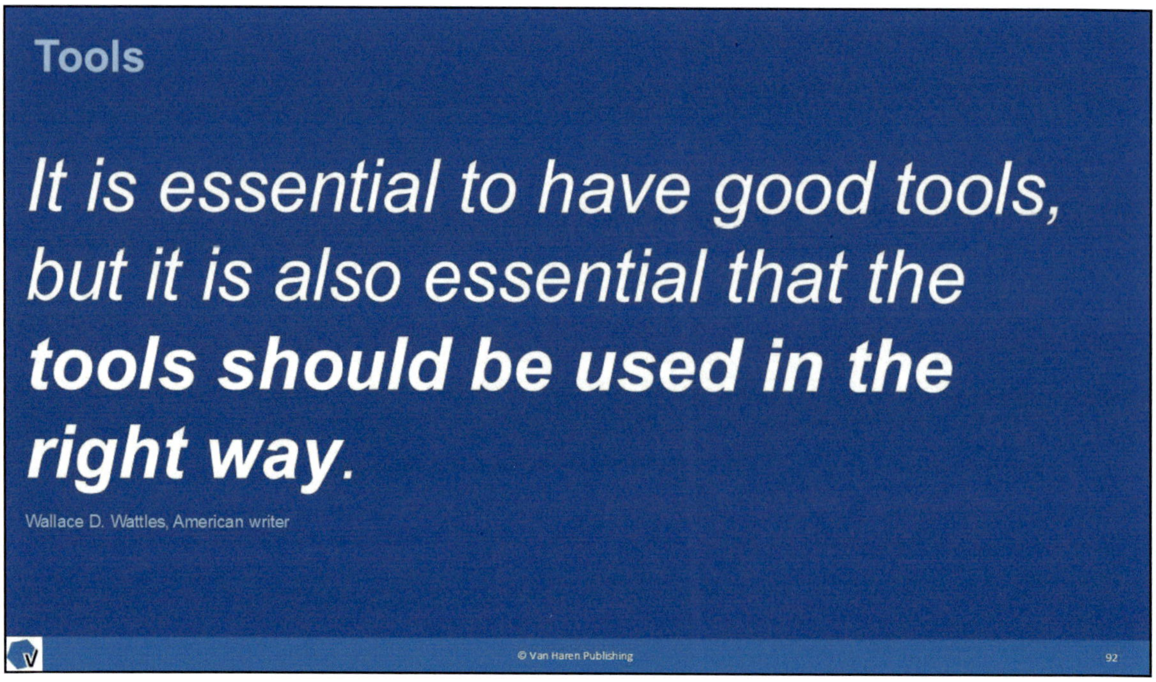
Tools
It is essential to have good tools, but it is also essential that the **tools should be used in the right way.**
Wallace D. Wattles, American writer
© Van Haren Publishing
92

Tools

Data Modeling Tools
Drawing data models, forward engineering, backward engineering.

Lineage Tools
Track the flow of data over time. Impact analysis.

Data Profiling Tools
Explore and validate data content and assess Data Quality.

Metadata Repositories
Storing and sharing of descriptive information about the data model.

Data Model Patterns
Reusable modeling structures on elementary, assembly and integration data model patterns.

Industry Data Models
Pre-built models for an entire industry. Broad and detailed. Must be customizable.

 93

Governance

We cannot be mere consumers of good governance, we must be participants; ***we must be co-creators.***

Rohini Nilekani, Indian writer and philanthropist

 94

Data Model Governance
Develop Standards
Review Design Quality
Versioning & Integration
© Van Haren Publishing
95

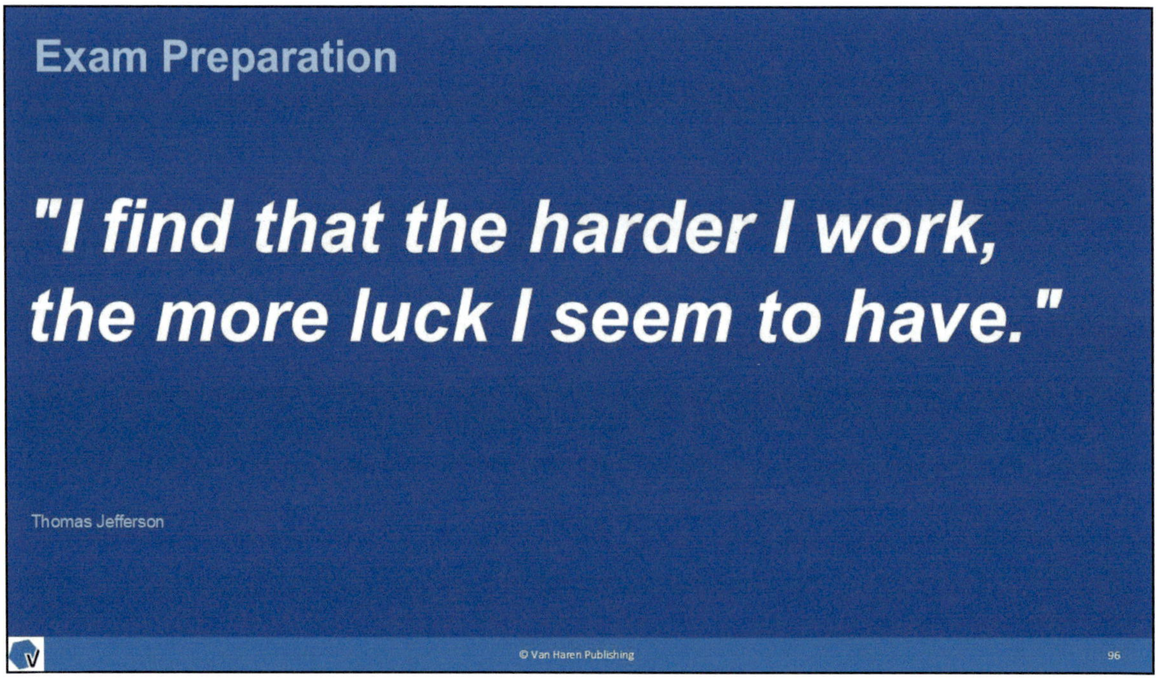
Exam Preparation
"I find that the harder I work, the more luck I seem to have."
Thomas Jefferson
© Van Haren Publishing
96

Certification

ASSOCIATE	PRACTITIONER	MASTER	FELLOW
CDMP Associate	CDMP Practitioner	CDMP Master	CDMP Fellow
Membership Central	Membership Central	Membership Central	Membership Central
Industry experience 6 months > 5 years	Industry experience 2 years - 10 years	Industry experience Minimum 10 years^	Industry experience 25 years plus
Requirements 60% pass Data Management Fundamentals exam	Requirements 70% pass in Data Management Fundamentals exam and 70% pass in 2 specialist exams	Requirements 80% pass in Data Management Fundamentals exam and 80% pass in 2 specialist exams	Requirements Globally recognised & respected thought leadership Significant contribution to Data Management profession CDMP Master Contribution to CDMP & DMBOK By nomination

 97

Example question

1. What are relationship labels?

A. The verb phrases describing the business rules in each direction between two entities.
B. The nullability setting on a foreign key.
C. A foreign key that has been role-named.
D. A relationship without cardinality.
E. A non-identifying relationship.

 98

Example question

2. Which of these statements has the most meaningful relationship label?

A. An order line contains orders.
B. An order is associated with order lines.
C. An order is related to order lines.
D. An order is connected with order lines.
E. An order is composed of order lines.

 99

Example question

3. All of the following are TRUE statements on relationship types except:

A. A many-to-many relationship says that an instance of each entity may be associated with many instances of the other entity, and vice versa.
B. A one-to-one relationship says that a parent entity may have one and only one child entity.
C. A one-to-many relationship says that a parent entity may have one or more child entities.
D. A one-to-many relationship says that a child entity may have one or more parent entities.
E. A recursive relationship relates instances of an entity to other instances of the same entity.

 100

Example question

4. In the BASE vs ACID model for Transaction Processing, "E" is best described which of these statements?

A. End to End data consistency
B. Eventual Availability of Data as described by the CAP theorem
C. Eventual Data Consistency
D. Extra Validation
E. Business Availability of Secure data ELEMENTS

Example question

5. A bank applies the business rule that each Customer may own one or many Accounts and each Account must be owned by one or many Customers. Which relationship type would be most appropriate?

A. many-to-many.
B. one-to-many.
C. many-to-one.
D. one-to-one.
E. recursive.

Example question

6. An employee may work for one other employee and may manage one or more employees. There is an indeterminate number of levels in this management hierarchy. What type of relationship would work best?

A. recursive.
B. one-to-one.
C. subtyping.
D. identifying.
E. non-identifying.

 103

Example question

7. Which of the following business rules should NOT appear on a logical data model?

A. Each Person can work for zero to many Companies
B. Customer Last Name requires a non-unique index to improve retrieval performance.
C. Each Company must employ one or many Persons.
D. Each Order can contain one or many Order Lines.
E. Each Policy must belong to one Policy Owner.

 104

Example question

8. All of the following are properties of a logical data model except:

A. contains relationship cardinality
B. technology-independent
C. contains attributes
D. contains primary keys
E. technology-dependent

Example question

9. The purpose for adding redundancy to a data model (denormalisation) is to:

A. optimise overall database performance across both data access and data update requests.
B. fully utilise all the indexes.
C. avoid the loss of data by storing key values more than once.
D. ensure surrogate keys are retaining their unique values in all satellite tables.
E. make it easier for developers to join tables.

Example question

10. A project scope includes the collection, exchange and reporting of data from multiple systems. Conceptual, logical and physical data models are maintained. How many models of each type can be expected?

A. More physical data models than logical data models, and more logical data models than conceptual data models.
B. More logical data models than physical data models, and more logical data models than conceptual data models.
C. More conceptual data models than logical data models, and more logical data models than physical data models.
D. The same number of each of the model types.
E. Only 1 conceptual data model, 1 logical data model and 1 physical data model.

 107

Example question

11. Which of the following is NOT true of a super-type/sub-type entity relationship?

A. Attributes and relationships shared by some, but not all, sub-types are modelled with the sub-types
B. Sub-type entities must be mutually exclusive
C. A sub-type inherits all attributes and relationships of the super-type
D. Attributes and relationships shared by all sub-types are modelled with the super-type
E. The Subtype relationships should have a discriminator attribute

 108

Example question

12. DMBoK2 identifies the best definition of cardinality as the following:

A. An entity and its attributes
B. How many of one entity participates in the relationship with how many (i.e. instances) of another entity
C. The number of entities attached to other entities
D. The distinction between the attributes and their interrelated entities
E. The relationship is either mandatory or optional

Example question

13. Data Lineage Tools are used to:

A. Capture CDM to LDM to PDM Mapping
B. Capture change in domain data over time
C. Capture changes in data model over time
D. Capture data flow from source systems to data warehouse or data mart
E. Capture and maintenance of the source structures for each attribute on the data model

Example question

14. Which of the following is a true statement when completing the initial Conceptual Data Model (CDM)?

A. Capture the enterprise viewpoint
B. Capture each individual viewpoint
C. Capture how a viewpoint fits within the organization as a whole
D. Capture how a viewpoint fits with other departments
E. Capture the viewpoint of the user group

 111

Example question

15. In a data model in which COURSE has a one-to-many relationship to itself and COURSE, STUDENT and SEMESTER are foreign keyed to REGISTRATION table, the REGISTRATION table has relationship:

A. Nullary
B. Ternary
C. Factorial
D. Unary
E. Binary

 112

Example question

16. What is the type of model that is used by an organization to standardize the common messaging format for data sharing?

A. Physical
B. Dimensional
C. Canonical
D. Data Vault
E. Service Oriented Architecture

Example question

17. The Data Vault Modelling is a hybrid approach, encompassing the best of breed between:

A. 3NF and star schema
B. Physical and Logical Model
C. Time based and Anchor Modelling
D. UML and ORM
E. 4NF and snowflake

Example question

18. All of the following are benefits of normalization except:

A. Removes derived data
B. Removes repeating attributes
C. Removes non-key attributes
D. Removes attribute redundancies
E. Removes attribute hidden dependencies

Example question

19. Which of the following business rules should NOT appear on a logical data model?

A. Each Policy must belong to one Policy Owner
B. Customer Last Name requires a non-unique index to improve retrieval performance
C. Each Person can work for zero to many Companies
D. Each Company must employ one or many Persons
E. Each Order can contain one or many Order Lines

Example question - Answers

1.	A	11.	B
2.	E	12.	B
3.	D	13.	A
4.	C	14.	E
5.	A	15.	B
6.	A	16.	C
7.	B	17.	A
8.	E	18.	C
9.	A	19.	B
10.	A		

 117